*Book Given to
David Perry Grosse
by Mom
Willowdean A. 'Sill' Grosse*

HOW ARE YOU DOING?

Journal Of A Dead Man Born Again

By
David Paul Garty

*Son of David H. Garty
Rev.

Love in Christ*

1

Scripture taken from the Holy Bible, NEW INTERNATIONAL VERSION © copyright 1973, 1978, 1984 by International Bible Society. Used by permission of Zondervan Publishing House. All rights reserved.
The "NIV" and "New International Version" trademarks are registered in the United States Patent and Trademark Office by International Bible Society. Use of either trademark requires the permission of International Bible Society.

Scripture taken from the NEW AMERICAN STANDARD BIBLE ®, (NASB) Copyright © 1960, 1962, 1963, 1968, 1971, 1972, 1973, 1975, 1977, 1995 by The Lockman Foundation. Used by permission.

Copyright © 2010 David Paul Garty
All rights reserved. No part of this book or cover may be reproduced in any form without written permission from the author and publisher.

How Are You Doing? Journal of a Dead Man Born Again
By David Paul Garty

ISBN-10: 0-9742432-7-2
ISBN-13: 978-0-9742432-7-6

Cover design by Jillian Rowley

Flying Scroll Publishing, LLC
P.O. Box 246
Fort Atkinson, WI 53538
www.flyingscrollpublishing.com

Acknowledgements

I dedicate this book to God who keeps reminding me that the mercies of the Lord are new every morning.

I thank my parents and my brothers with their families for never giving up on me.

To the men, women, and children who have crossed my path at some point over the past forty years, I offer my gratitude for the impact you have made on my life.

Terrie Knox, my editor and friend; without your prayerful insights I would still be somewhere around page thirty wondering what I am going to do with all these things. Thank you!

And a big thanks also to my high school classmates who read over my initial manuscript and returned to me extremely valuable advice.

Finally, a big hug and a little peck on the cheek to my beautiful, six year old niece Jessie who took the time to draw a picture for me to use on the cover. And to Jillian Rowley for her expertise in doing so.

Preface

In the months which followed my awakening from a coma, several individuals encouraged me to write a book. Eagerly I began. My thoughts flowed more freely when I wrote letters to actual people, the first of which was addressed to a young woman who, to this day I have never met. My story was disclosed to her through a college roommate, who had dated one of my brothers in high school. Hearing the dramatic details brought tears to her eyes, or so I was told. It was communicated to me that her body had been hit by an out-of-control automobile while she and a friend walked home from their school one night. Her friend was critically injured. The forceful impact and the resulting flight through the air were still fresh in her remembrance. She divulged that she felt as though her body had been protected. As I understood it, a broken nose from the initial contact was the only personal injury which she reported as having significance. Her request for my testimony in writing was made known to me through my brother, who also gave me her address. It was the description of her tears which prompted my written response.

So began my journey. I was learning how to prayerfully express the deep things which were bottled-up inside me. Within the year's time between my life-changing accident and my starting to record thoughts in ink, I asked God to share with me how He saw my life. My introductory connotations were short lived. Though I am a main character in this narrative, it is really about God. My strongest aspiration for those who choose to pore over these pages is to find the eyes of their heart gazing Godward.

The words in the Bible are a good place to continue seeking God. The book of John in the NIV, chapter 7 and verse 37 ends with Jesus saying, *"If anyone is thirsty, let him come to me and drink."*

The word thirsty has made an impression on me. When we naturally thirst, it is not that we are going around trying to find something to drink. Being thirsty is feeling a realization of a need. We may go around and try to find something to drink when we are thirsty, but the going around part is not the thirst. The thirst is the realization of the need. You have the need and then you go looking.

Jesus said if anyone is thirsty. He was saying if anyone recognizes their felt need. So what is the need that He was talking about? Was He talking about mankind recognizing their need for God? He goes on to say, then come to Me and drink. He was saying that He has what we need, whatever it may be.

On an individual, every day basis it could be said that He was saying, whatever you have need of, come to Me and I have for you… Jesus is able to identify with our daily needs. Though He is God, the Son of God, He did not count equality with God as something to be grasped. He humbled himself. He came to this earth and took on the likeness of man. Was I hearing God say to me through His written word that when we recognize our felt needs, whatever they may be in this life, we are to come to Jesus in faith, to ask of Him and to receive? This is what I think that I was hearing. What do you think?

The first part of the definition for the word, 'thirst,' in the Webster dictionary is, 'bodily need of drink.' The second part of the definition is, 'an ardent desire or craving for something.' I am convinced in my heart that the basic need should not be overlooked. The definition for the word thirsty is, 'feeling thirst.' It is a feeling.

Jesus didn't say if you have thirst come and drink. He said if you are thirsty. He was saying if you feel your need. He wants us to know that He cares about our feelings. He wants us to know that He can identify with our feelings. He came to show us the way to God; the best way to deal with our feelings, the best way to fill the lack which is being recognized.

David Paul Garty
May 2010

Contents

Twelve Steps	Page	8
How Are You Doing?	Page	14
Head-On Into A Semi	Page	16
A Mother's Heart	Page	18
After Seven Days	Page	24
A Life Of Sowing Seeds	Page	27
A Life Of Purpose	Page	30
Good News	Page	34
God's Way	Page	36
Hope In The Lord	Page	40
Hope With Me, Pray With Me	Page	42
What Is Better	Page	51
A Struggle For Power	Page	58
In Search Of The Fear Of The Lord	Page	67
Finding Direction	Page	72
A Step In Obedience	Page	77
Deferred Hope	Page	81
Precious	Page	85
A Moral Inventory	Page	96
From Whence Didst Thou Come?	Page	101

Twelve Steps

Through the process of growing up and maturing over the years, there have been many times when I've been convinced that I cannot make it on my own. I need others and the insights which they provide. While celebrating my recovery a few years ago, I was asked to share my testimony based on the "Twelve Steps and Their Biblical Comparisons" from Rick Warren's "Celebrate Recovery." Our testimonies grow as we grow and mature in this life. The words which follow are the words I shared at that time.

My name is David. I am a believer who struggles with hurts, habits and hang-ups. These things in my life have had the names of fear, depression, and suicide as well as drug and alcohol abuse. I must also call the fleshly, sexual lust which so easily entangles my mind, exactly the hang-up that it is.

What was the insanity of my life before recovery? Before realizing that I am not God and choosing to admit that I am powerless to control my own tendency to do wrong and before acknowledging that my life was not manageable, I tried to hide or cover up the emptiness inside me by withdrawing and turning away from any truth that had previously been revealed to me. But I found that only God can fill that emptiness by His Spirit through the living Word of God. Running around in the same old circles of sin only led me to hate life. There is no hope in these circles. They just bring me down. The lack of faith that is behind these circles, lack of faith in the only true God, led me to death.

Before believing whole-heartedly that God exists, that I do matter to Him, and that He does have the power to help me recover, I had heard there was a God who loved me. I had even asked His Son, Jesus to come into my heart and life when I was a boy. Through life's challenges and my choosing to not walk in forgiveness, God remained what other people believed and He seemed way far away from me.

Seeing God as far away affected my attitude and relationship toward others. I withdrew into my own little world with all its fear and pain. I didn't believe anyone could help me or even had any idea how to help if they could or would try to imagine. I tried to be nice to people like I was taught as a child but when other people's plans were different than mine, I just went back to my own little world and didn't let anyone see the me who was afraid or hurt.

Near the age of thirteen years old, I remember being up in my bedroom telling God that I didn't want to hurt Him, but I couldn't deal with everything that was going on around me. Not long after, I was introduced to a controlled substance by a youth who I was growing up with. That got the ball rolling to my bottom line at age twenty.

I used to play suicidal games like riding my Sportster at over one hundred mph in the wrong lane, head-on at semi's and waiting to see how close I could get before leaning to miss the collision. I carried hurts in my heart from my past that I did not know how to deal with. I believed that

I needed to talk to someone, but I did not feel as though I had the freedom internally to talk to anyone.

Then one day, I had a wild thought in the form of a question. Somehow God, whom I had asked into my heart when I was a boy and later walked away from, was in my thoughts asking me how I was doing. I was so intrigued by the thought that I went outside to answer Him under the guise of restocking everyone with a beer. I looked up at the sky and walked around the yard. I felt as though I was telling God how I felt.

I told Him I hated the life I had known because of the church split when people tried to break up my family. I told Him I hated the life which I was living because I was going no where except around in the same old circles. Then I asked Him if He had another world. I told Him how I thought it would take a crash into a semi before I would believe there was something different for me.

With a hard heart like that, how did I get into recovery? I had tried to make changes in my life by taking a membership at a health club and I began running. These external changes felt good at times, but they did not change my heart. Lifting weights did not give me the internal fortitude to make right choices. I needed more than a change in my outward appearance.

God did not forget our conversation when I actually did crash into a semi. Even though my entire lower jaw was broken in pieces and smashed out the back of my head, even though one of my lungs was deflated leaving me unable to breathe on my own, and even though I had numerous other injuries, was in a coma and not expected to live, I awoke from that coma one week later with a revelation of God's reality. I believed that He did care about me. My jaw had been reconstructed by surgeons but through prayers of faith by believers in Jesus Christ, my lung, my stomach, and my leg were healed by God.

Even after such an awesome experience of God's love and power, there were times when doubt and shame overcame me. Over the next ten or so years I was given chance after chance to believe in God's life for me without it having to take a semi crash. I would fall into what seemed the pits of hell. There was more than one time when I woke up in a hospital emergency room after drinking so much Tequila that my body completely shut down. Once, I was told that I had quit breathing. I imagine my breathing had stopped on more than one of these occasions. But through these tests and trials, God remained faithful through His gentle and loving discipline. To what more than God's faithfulness can I give credit? Through them all, God kept waking me up.

Do the tests ever end? They didn't when I moved to Texas after walking out of the hospital for the last time. A new offer was made to me in the Lone-Star state. All the times I had used drugs or alcohol, among other things, to forget my own little world, I felt I was only hurting myself. When a proposition was spoken to me about smuggling marijuana into the country through a member of the Mexican Mafia who I had become acquainted with, I started thinking about all of the kids and other people who could be hurt by me. Thinking of others as more important than myself in this situation finally led me to lay down my addiction and walk away from it.

    Getting into recovery has been a process with me that started with a head-on crash with a semi. I had to choose to abandon myself and consciously commit all my life and will to Christ's care and control. Through each test and trial, I have had to consciously choose to re-commit my life and will to Christ. It is something I have to do continually each day. This is a process that has stayed with me through the years only because of God's grace. My own will power has never been enough to save me.

    God, in His faithfulness, continues to bring His Word to life in me by His Spirit. That is how my recovery is influenced. Fellowship with God and those who believe in God's Word is a true gift. He has been making changes in my relationships with others. For one, I talk to people now ... at least a little bit.

    I believe God has shown me that I need to do three things in my recovery. 1.) I need to forgive. 2.) I need to let go of any resentments or bitterness. 3.) I need to make myself vulnerable to new friendships. Growing up through all my teenage years with un-forgiveness, resentments, and being withdrawn from practically everyone, I did not learn to be much of a social person. God promises He will continue the work He has begun in us so maybe someday I'll talk your ear off.

    One day, I was sitting in a Boom-truck at a gas station taking a quench my thirst break. I had hauled a couple bunks of drywall up some stairs in a new house being built down the road from there. I looked out the side window to watch a car roll up beside me. I saw what appeared to be the passenger putting pot into a paper to roll a joint. When the driver noticed that I saw what they were doing, his eyes got really big. I imagined that he felt like he was busted. He pulled the car up further, out of my sight. I thought, "Wow, I used to do that." I'm glad I don't have to do that or feel like that any more. My only Rescuer is Christ and what He did for me on the cross. God raised Him from the dead, sent His Holy Spirit to help us recover through God's Word and puts us in a fellowship of believers to keep His Word around us.

How has my walk with God changed? God is not just something that other people believe in anymore. He is real to me now and I believe He has the power to help me recover. I don't always feel like I matter to Him, but in my spirit I know that I do. In Christ, I can walk by faith and not by sight.

Feeling safe and being convinced that I am worth something is far better to me than the pain and fear of my past. I now can trust that I am accepted right where I am yet I am spiritually drawn to be changed even more as I put on my new identity in Christ. I am finally realizing that my deepest needs are met in Him.

But let's start at the beginning...

How Are You Doing?

In the fall of 1990, a thought caught my attention; it came in the form of a question. It seemed as though someone had asked me how I was doing. With an amazing sense of intrigue, I walked around outside for several minutes while I searched for an answer.

If anyone had seen me, they may have classified me as a "nut." I was staring up into the sky and conversing with myself. Honestly, it did not matter to me what anyone thought at that moment. The question which was raised seemed sincere. In my opinion, a respectful answer was due.

I was convinced in my heart that the living God, who I had learned of and asked to come into my heart while in my childhood, was right there in my thoughts. For nearly eight years prior to this vivid encounter, I did not recall much reality of His presence. In my mind, the God who I had previously believed in was far off and not interested in me. But at this juncture, I accepted as truth in my heart that God had asked me, "How are you doing?" So I told Him. I told Him how I felt.

"I cannot imagine a life other than living with the hurt I have already experienced," I said, and "I cannot see one reason to continue living." I continued, "Even though I cannot imagine a better life, if You have another life for me, will You bring me into Your world?" Ignorantly, I then told God how I believed it would have to happen. "It is going to take something like a semi," I explained, with a head-on crash in mind. For a moment I surrendered my own will and asked for help. Then, I went back inside and pondered what had just happened. Though my memory did not hang onto the encounter for long, God did not forget.

Head-On Into A Semi

The morning of January 5th, 1991 arrived as the clock finished dinging midnight from the day before. My intention was to celebrate the New Year with a few former high school classmates, some of whom were on break from college. We did what we had grown up doing. We attempted to alter our minds and escape reality through drugs and alcohol. But I grew restless.

In my drunken state, I began to dwell on vows which I had made to myself in the previous years. The first vow was that I would never again consume strong drink. From the time I had left active duty in the armed forces until that night I had kept that vow. Agitated with myself, I feared losing my self-control; I feared I might lash out at others. A second commitment which I had made as a boy neared being broken as well.

The remembrance of seeing the imprint of a grown man's fist embedded in my skin had always prevented me from wanting to hit anyone else. The mark did not go away for days. I knew what it was to hurt and I purposed in my heart never to hit anyone or cause someone else to feel what I had felt. Earlier in the evening, I had almost lost that measure of self-control. So I made another attempt to distance myself from the temptation.

Intoxicated, I went for a drive. It had been common throughout my teen years to go for long drives. But I did not make it to the back-country roads that night as I usually did. I do remember getting into the car and backing out of the driveway. I do recall that my state of mind was not very healthy. However, recollection evades me as to whether I actually saw the stop sign or the lights of the tractor-trailer as I neared impact.

The police report states that a Ford, Tempo was driven through a stop sign at nearly 40 miles per hour and ran head-on into a commercial vehicle while crossing highway US-12. I can only relay the details that were given to me about the accident itself.

I was told I had to be cut out of the vehicle. At one point they had to pump oxygen into my one remaining functional lung. The mechanism was described to me as a type of billows like what is used to pump air into a fire. A part of the car gouged bone and flesh from my right lower extremity causing the leg to lose its stability for standing. My right arm was broken near the wrist again for the third time in twenty years.

These injuries along with minor cuts and bruises seemed pale in comparison to my mandible being broken in many places and smashed out the back of my head behind the right ear. This caused a great deal of swelling. I was flown to a large city hospital by helicopter and hooked up to a machine to keep me breathing. My parents were told that it could be six months to one year before I would wake up… if I woke up at all.

A Mother's Heart

My mother's writings while I was in a coma follow:

01-07-91

Saturday, about 3:10 a.m., we received a call from Sturgis Hospital that David was there in the emergency room due to a motor vehicle accident. His father, his brother Mike, and I quickly dressed and went immediately to the emergency room, which is approximately 5 to 6 blocks from our home. When arriving, we were able to see David after the attending physician explained to us his condition of a broken jaw, arm, and leg. He also had a possible brain (head) injury. The helicopter from Bronson Methodist Hospital was on its way to pick him up to take him to the Trauma Unit at Bronson Hospital.

David had multiple cuts on his face, arms, legs, and chest. A deep laceration on his right cheek and lower right leg was evident. He was being assisted with oxygen. Though he was able to breathe on his own, his breathing was more shallow than necessary to get enough oxygen to lungs and brain. We were informed the oxygen was necessary, especially in lieu of a head injury. It was important that oxygen get to the brain cells. Because a respirator also has a vacuum process, it helps to keep excess fluids off the lungs which can cause pneumonia.

David was flown by helicopter and was attended by a trauma team while aboard. He was sent immediately for CT testing upon arrival at Bronson Methodist Hospital. These tests showed no spinal damage and no bleeding in his brain, thanks to God, but did show swelling which occurs in head injuries and damage can result from that. We continue to trust the Lord. His face (lower part) and neck were quite swollen- normal the doctors say from such an injury. His vital signs have remained stable. The nurses say they are keeping watch out for infection, especially in his leg. The cut went deep to his bone and cut a chip off the bone. It has been stitched with a small section left open for drainage if necessary. The smaller bone in the right arm was broken toward the wrist area. It is in a splint at this time as David could injure it further when he flails his arms around. The thrashing is the body's way of saying it's hurting, but David is not out of the coma and communicating.

At 12:30 a.m., Sunday morning, the nurse gave David command signals again (to lift two fingers and wiggle toes) and he responded. It is a positive sign that the pressure on the brain is decreasing. Later that morning, he responded to his dad and me by opening his eyes when his dad called to him. We have since seen positive command movement and are encouraged. He still sleeps a lot due to the swelling, but has awakened at times He cannot talk as the oxygen tube goes through the voice box area. His movements tell us he feels pain.

It's after 11 a.m., January 7, and we see that <u>some</u> swelling is down from his neck and face. The doctors may do surgery today to repair his jaw which is broken in two places under the lip and crushed higher up in the face area. The eye socket bones do not appear to be broken. The blow was so hard on his lower face that the broken bones protruded through the skin behind his right ear. The plastic surgeon hopes to be able to place a metal plate in David's jaws to hold it for healing. If not, he will have to wire David's jaws together. This would have to stay in for 6-8 weeks. These injuries take time for healing.

We are keeping our faith that David will continue to progress. Many family members of those also in the Trauma area say their loved ones progressed and then had set backs. Each patient is different of course, and David's nurses have said that when someone shows improvement in the first 24 hours as David has, there is continued progress from then on out. We realize he's still under the coma and pressure still seems to be on his brain from swelling, but signs from him are giving us hope.

It is 1:45 p.m. and we are in the waiting room. The afternoon nurse for David just came in to have us sign a form allowing them to put the IV in through his upper chest to give him nutrients. She said that the veins in the arm are thin and easy to collapse so moving the IV to an area close to the artery would be better for him.

The Dr. has not been in yet today as he probably has office calls first. We are waiting to hear what he says regarding the time for David's surgery.

The nurses have only had to give David two grams of morphine when needed (about once every 3-4 hours). They chose not to give him any earlier this afternoon at the usual time as David was resting peaceably. But about 1 p.m.,

David was thrashing as in pain, so four grams were administered at that time. According to the nurse, two grams is a very low amount compared to amounts that other patients need. So we are pleased he has been able to tolerate his condition without heavy continued sedation. Oh, I remember now. He was in discomfort because they are lowering the amount of oxygen they are giving him so he will breathe more on his own. This was a bit of a surprise to his system and that's the discomfort that helped the nurse decide to up the grams of morphine. Keep praying!

The Dr. just told us he foresees David's surgery to be Wednesday. He is pretty sure David may be given a tracheotomy to help with breathing while his mouth is wired together… a nurse came to see us to sign for David to have a tube put in his side to release an air pocket that developed between his lung and ribs. This was due to the accident and necessary to release so it would not grow and collapse his lung.

01-08-91
Back at the hospital again, shortly after 8 a.m. We checked on David and he had rested well. He had not been given medication since 5:30 a.m. Dave, Mike, and Jarrett went back to Sturgis to take care of insurance and other such things. At 11 a.m., I went in to be with David. I met the physical therapist who will work with David to keep joints limber and muscles working. Also, the nurse said David responded during his bath by lifting his leg and arm when asked. She gave him his first medication (at 10:00) since 5:30 a.m.; after his bath he seemed to be feeling some pain/discomfort. She was pleased to see his progress. I have decided to get some lunch.

Dave and Mike arrived back about 3 p.m. Others from the church came in around 4 p.m. and had prayer with us. David responded with his eyes and a squeeze of hand. He seemed to be trying to voice something. He cannot talk, however, due to the tube through his voice box area. He seemed to gag a little and I stayed with him holding his hand till he relaxed. Mike stayed with me while Dave walked out with the others... we went out to eat with them. When we returned, David was resting. We stayed again at the Hospitality House.

01-09-91

7 a.m., we came to the hospital as David was to have surgery on his jaw at 9 a.m. While visiting David, the nurse said an emergency surgery patient came in and they will hold off on David until the afternoon. Then the surgical neurologist checked on David. Although he responded earlier this morning to commands from the nurse, the doctor did not feel David's responses were as good as Monday. David may be tired from earlier workout. He has come a long way so far. We pray and trust God.

The surgery was moved to 1 o'clock, then to 3 p.m. and finally at 4 p.m. he was taken to repair the jaw. The waiting is long. It is 6:25 p.m. now and we've not gotten word yet... the nurse said it would be two hours, maybe three and the surgeon would talk to us before David was taken back to the Trauma Unit for recovery. Then it will be a couple of hours before we can see him.

About a half hour or so before being taken to surgery, David had one of the reactions about which we were warned.

Dave was going in to see him and he was sitting up in bed- his legs over the side trying to get out of bed and his nurse trying to get him to lie down and keep his tube in his mouth. This nurse was a small lady and David was much stronger. Dave helped and David fought him too, placing his feet in Dave's chest and pushing. Remember, this is normal reaction and David is not in conscious control. He may have more of these incidences. It's better than him not moving at all.

At about 7 p.m. the Dr. finished with David and came to let us know that surgery went well. The nurse let us in to see him about a half hour later. Vital signs are good. Dave, Mike, and I are going home for the night and must make many calls as people want to know how he's coming along. Dave has some business to do in the morning and I need to do some laundry.

01-10-91
    Dave called at 8 a.m. The nurse said he woke up about 9 last night and fought a little. It is a good sign. We've had several calls and visitors checking to see how David is doing...

After Seven Days

One of the Sunday-school teachers that had taught me in my childhood prayed that Jesus would visit me in my coma. Believers in Jesus, who joined in prayer with her and my parents, prayed in that way also.

The doctors had explained to my parents that there was a possibility I may never awaken. In practicality, they also faced the possibility that I would never again be able to remember who I was. Some doctors highlighted the potential that I would never walk again.

Yet, after seven days, I gained consciousness. My first remembrance upon awakening was hearing my dad's voice. He inquired of me though I have not held onto the initial words he spoke. I only remember the first words which came from my mouth following the seven days in a coma.

My response to my dad's inquiry was, "I am not who you think I am."

He questioned, "Who do you think you are?"

"I am a ball of light!" was my reply. I cried deeply as I welcomed Jesus to take control of my life again. I could not see Jesus or feel him physically, but in my heart I knew that He was real.

When I was near ten years old, I had asked Jesus to be the Lord and Savior of my life. I was baptized in water at that young age. God proved to me that He had neither left me nor forsaken me even when I had walked away from my faith in Him for many years. Being raised as a pastor's son, I had heard many times that God is light; there is no darkness in Him. The revelation of God's purity was brought to life in my spirit through experiencing His presence within me while lying in the hospital bed.

On more than one occasion in the hospital following the reconstruction of my lower jaw, doctors found that my body was being healed miraculously after my parents and other believers in Jesus would pray for me. To inflate the lung which had collapsed, a tube had been inserted through the side of my chest. When the tube was removed, there was a concern for the lung to stay inflated. It was also necessary for the hole in my side to close properly. Through prayer in the name of Jesus, this healing took place before the doctor's planned operation to do the same.

Three other specific areas which needed attention were an infection in the leg that had been damaged, a staff infection which I had contracted while in the hospital, and the restored use of my stomach and waste elimination system. These problematic areas were addressed by prayer in faith. Every one was met with health and wholeness within twenty-four to forty-eight hours after approaching God's throne of grace.

No one seems able to recognize that my lower jaw is enforced by metal designed to stabilize the bone fragments. My other injuries are also mostly undetectable by the majority of people. However, I am reminded of it all whenever I play golf.

Remembering that my right arm was not supposed to be broken, my body grew another bone to fill in the crack. With the new growth attaching itself to both the ulna and radius bones, I am unable to twist my right wrist. I am not a professional golfer, but it is my understanding that twisting the wrist when swinging a golf club can cause the ball to slice off in an unwanted direction. Not being able to twist my wrist has helped me to hit the golf ball straighter.

One week after my awakening, the staff at the hospital said that I could go home; that there wasn't anything wrong with me. They said that what had taken place with me over this brief span of time had never been seen before in that facility. Amazingly, the chunk of bone gouged from my right lower leg was replaced by new bone growth almost immediately. Within the first week after awakening from the coma, I walked through the hospital halls on this leg which was damaged, without a cast or crutches. I had been asked to stay for one more week only so they could observe me.

Some hospital staff members called me, "the miracle." I feel that I am only an extension of the greatest miracle which ever happened. The good news of Jesus Christ is the miraculous force of God for the deliverance, healing, safety, and soundness of everyone who believes.

A Life of Sowing Seeds

Soon after returning home from the hospital following the semi-accident I went to a church meeting. There was a guest from Canada who was speaking to the church. I was asked to walk up to the front of the room. This man shared some words with me which he believed were directly from God. One of the words which he prophetically spoke is that I would carry a seed bag. This word is one that has remained with me.

Over the next several years, I read a few books in my longing to know God better. As I read, I would also copy down on my own paper the words which stood out to me. I did this to easily access the thoughts which I believed God had highlighted. The book entitled, "The Believer's Secret Of Intercession," compiled from the writings of Andrew Murray and CH Spurgeon by Lewis Gifford Parkhurst, Jr inspired me to pray in new ways and to copy down the words from my own heart that I prayerfully sensed. They are as follows:

...pray for each other... (James 5.16 NIV)

Praying is something that we should do. Out of realization that God is on our side and that there are many people in our daily lives who God desires to share His love with, we should pray. Joining together with others in prayer yields a special strength that can be felt. Jesus himself made a promise concerning agreement in prayer.

Again, I tell you that if two of you on earth agree about anything you ask for, it will be done for you by my Father in heaven. (Matthew 18:19 NIV)

We need each other, not just in external fellowship, but in approaching God for the sake of others. Abraham and Moses practiced intercession for others and through their faith in action by prayer they accomplished seemingly impossible results.

My heart cries out: Great and awesome God, in comparison to people like Abraham and Moses, I am very small in my own thinking. They succeeded in ways that are difficult for me to even imagine. Yet I think of Your Son, Jesus. He promised even greater things for those who believe in Him.

I tell you the truth, anyone who has faith in me will do what I have been doing. He will do even greater things than these, because I am going to the Father.
(John 14:12 NIV)

Help me to intercede for others. Show me how to pray the things that are on Your heart and encourage me with many wonderful answers to prayer.

My Lord and my God, thank You for the prayers that Christ prays for me. Help me to join Him in His prayers for others. Help me to be more concerned for the benefit of others than for myself. Give to me revelation and insight into the hurting hearts of others. Speak to me Your words of life and healing that I may share with them and help them to heal.

In his book, Parkhurst wrote about seeds. He described sowing seeds by explaining that even a weak person can put a seed into the ground. He also shared the idea that it is not the hard work of putting the seed into the ground that makes things grow. "It is the vitality of the seed," he wrote. It is like this when praying in faith. "When you can plead a promise and drop that prayer into the ground with faith, your weakness shall not make it futile," he went on to declare.

It is neither the one who puts the seeds into the ground nor the one who brings in the final crops that gets the credit. It is God who causes things to grow. Thank You God for all of Your promises. As I search for Your promises recorded in the Bible, make me aware of how I may pray in faith for Your will to be done on earth as it is in heaven.

A Life Of Purpose

Twenty-one days after losing my life in the semi accident, I walked away from the hospital. I purposed in my heart to change my views and to accept the will of God for my life. I have not yet been made perfect, but one thing I am learning to do is to put behind me the things which have passed and to keep on keeping on. I walked away from the hospital purposing in my heart to live the life God brought me back to life to live.

The living God is no respecter of persons. Truly, He is faithful to His Word. I began to make myself available to Him, that He might bring His written Word to life in me. By seeking His promises in the process of acting in faith, my mind was being renewed with Biblical truths. God would perform His Word in my actual experiences as my prayers would arise to Him in accordance with His divine principles.

One example is of a time when I was returning home from the Dominican Republic. I had been given an opportunity by a pastor from that country, to travel there and stay with him and his family. Following a one month stay, it seemed right for me to proceed home. The return flight landed safely at the Newark, NJ International Airport. From there I was able to board a Greyhound bus.

The bus had a layover at a Philadelphia, PA station. It had been warm south of the border, though it was now November. At this time, it was quite cool in the eastern United States and I wasn't dressed appropriately. I went into the restroom to put on some warmer clothes.

The bathroom was void of others. As I was putting on my belt, another person walked in. He must have noticed that I was changing when he passed by and went to a sink. A moment later, he turned to me and asked, "Do you have another belt?"

I took a deep breath and thought to myself, "Here we go...." I looked him in the eyes and told him that I did not have another belt. But I offered him the one which I was putting on. Removing it from my waist, I held it out for him to take. He did take the belt and thanked me as he looped it around his waist. And then he left and I hurried to finish changing. All the while I thought, "That was strange." I went out to sit in an empty row of seats near the middle of the bus station.

Nearly an hour went by. The same man I gave the belt to walked up to me with a pizza box in his hands. He asked me if I wanted a piece. I was somewhat hungry so I said sure. He sat down next to me and we ate some pizza... and we talked.

It turned out that he was homeless. He was living at the bus station and working there for food. Verifying his story was not a concern. I just listened. He said that he had recently gotten out of prison where he had been for a number of years. According to him, no family members were in that area and he was by himself. When he was done sharing, he asked me some questions.

I shared all that was on my heart. I told him I had been down-and-out at a point in my life and drove a vehicle head-on into a semi. I shared how messed up I had been and how God stepped into my life and put the pieces back together. That is what I knew.

Before I was done answering his questions, he was in tears. He was more than sobbing; he cried hard and loud for a long time right there in the middle of the bus station. I could see that his continence changed and his voice softened. An amazing sense of God's presence was real to me at that moment. I prayed with a vision to help this man.

It did not feel right to me to just leave him there on his own. He had told me that he had family in the Lancaster area. I was heading in that direction, so I bought him a bus ticket and took him with me. He told me his name was Ray. I did not know exactly what to do, but I had a sense that I was supposed to do something more to help him.

We arrived at the Lancaster station early in the morning. While we were on the road, I had an impression. It was that I was supposed to rent a hotel room for the two of us. We stayed at the hotel for three days until he could be connected with some church people who I had met there. They helped me during the previous summer and I thought they might be able to help him.

On the third day at the hotel, Ray prayed with me and asked Jesus to come into his heart and life as his Lord. On that third day, I was able to get in contact with a man in the church. I knew that the people in this church had opened up their homes to help out homeless people before. They took Ray in and gave him a safe place to stay.

      It was time for me to buy another bus ticket and head home. Through this whole experience, I carried over one thousand dollars in cash in my pocket which I had taken with me on my travel south. At any point in time, I could have been thumped on the head, robbed, and left for dead. This realization strengthened my trust in God's provision and care.

      I drove back east the following year and tried to find Ray at a church meeting. According to the person who had taken him in, he had stayed for a number of months but hadn't been around in a long time. Out of nowhere, without him knowing that I was there, Ray showed up at the one church gathering where I was. Following the church assembly we were able to talk for a few minutes. That was just too cool. I understood him to say that he had gotten in contact with some member of his family in that area. He looked and sounded much better than when we had first met. To my sorrow, I have since lost contact with Ray.

Good News

Everyone has a story to tell. According to the Hebrew-Greek Key Word Study Bible, the Apostle Paul shared his story of good news with the Romans. This included the following declaration: "For I am not ashamed of the gospel, for it is the power of God for salvation to everyone who believes, to the Jew first and also to the Greek." (Romans 1:16, underlining mine)

1) gospel- a good message
2) power- *force* (lit. or fig.); spec. miraculous *power*
3) salvation- deliver or protect, health, heal, preserve, be (make) whole
4) believes- to have *faith* (in, upon, or with respect to, a person or thing); to *entrust* (espec. one's spiritual well-being to Christ); commit (to trust); persuasion, credence, reliance, constancy

Anymore, when I think about Romans 1:16, I repeat in my own mind: For I am not ashamed of the good news of Jesus Christ for it is the miraculous force of God for the deliverance, the healing, the safety, and the soundness of everyone who sticks with Christ like glue, who commits to Him with faith and trusts in and relies upon Him.

There was a time during the summer following my accident with the semi when I worked for a temporary job placement agency. They had placed me in the spare parts department of a company where the manufacturing of delivery vehicles took place. On a day like any other day, I was asked to band together a skid full of steel bumpers.

The banding for this particular assignment was a little different than other rolls of banding which I was accustomed to using. It was one and one quarter inches wide and required its own special crimping tools which were mounted on the cart. This increased the weight of the cart which already had a nearly full roll of banding on it.

Bending down on one knee, I looked under the skid to feed the banding underneath. It had run out of slack so I gave it a quick pull. Without warning, all the weight of the cart, the nearly full role of banding, together with the poundage of the crimping devices toppled over and smashed my head between it and a steel bumper. I felt the crushing blow on one side and the entrapment between metal on the other. I sensed a rush of adrenalin, but there was no pain.

One of the tow-motor drivers witnessed the incident. He raced over to me. To both of our amazement, I stood up unharmed. He expressed his concern that he thought he was going to have to call an ambulance. Save for a single drop of blood which stood on my right cheek from being poked by a tread that protruded from one of the pieces of steel, it was difficult to tell that anything unfavorable had happened. Immediately my heart and soul were flooded with thankfulness to God who had kept me safe. I remembered Paul's letter to the Romans written all those years ago. I was in awe at how those words had come to life in my present tense.

God's Way

Nearly one year after the crash with the semi, I had a desire to go on a walk toward the east coast to search for the Lord and His purpose for my life. I told my dad what I was contemplating. He did not respond immediately. The next day, he told me he had sought God in prayer and did not have peace with my planned adventure.

His attention was quickened by the thought of my camping at one of the two state parks which stood out in his memory. I surrendered my own way and submitted myself to my father's wishes. I believed God would work everything out for good. With peace, I made arrangements to stay near Warren Dunes on Lake Michigan to camp for the month of June in the summer of 1992.

Though I was bothered some by not being able to search for God in the way I first desired, He honored my submission to His principles and met with me. I sought Him with thanksgiving in my heart and with praise on my lips for the opportunity I was given. I began to learn the obedience of Christ as I suffered the release of my own will and desire.

I ended up pitching my tent across from the state park on the property known then as New Life Campground and Motel. As I settled into the campsite, I became acquainted with the owners of the property. It just so happened that these owners had just taken over the campground a few months before my arrival. I found out later that they also happened to be the aunt and uncle of one of my closest friends from high-school. The "buddy", with whom I had enlisted into the Army, is their nephew.

Devoting much of my time to memorizing and confessing God's promises and studying the teachings of Jesus that are recorded in the Bible, I asked God to bring His Word to life in my everyday experiences by His Spirit. As I began to commit my every thought, word and action to His Word, He met me where I was at and began changing me. My attitudes and motivations were being purified within me.

One afternoon, while at the campground store, I took notice that a wind storm had moved into the area. Concerned for my little pup-tent, I moved in the direction of my site to find the tent up in the air, flapping in the wind with only three remaining pegs securing it to the ground. Quickly grabbing onto the ropes, I struggled as the wind blew so hard I could barely hang on. The ropes slipped slowly out of my grip.

With all the excitement going on around me at that particular moment, I cannot imagine why I would have a thought to speak to the wind. However, that was the impression which came to me. I didn't know what else to do, so I took a chance. Can you imagine how hard my heart was beating as this thought blended into the condition I was faced with?

I cried aloud, "Father!" Then, after pausing for a moment, I thought OK. With the winds still whipping through the campgrounds, I shouted, "Wind, in the name of, Jesus, be gone!" All of a sudden a gentle stillness rested upon my campsite. All around the rest of the campground trees were still being blown over. With the stillness that surrounded my tent came peace and a fear of the Lord.

As my plan to walk across the country was changed to camping beside Lake Michigan, likewise my plan to be alone for an extended period of time was interrupted by people. In one way or another, though, I did learn many things from the people God brought to my path.

Two young children come to my remembrance. They were sister and brother. Both were under the age of ten years. They lived at the campground with their parents for the summer. The children used to walk around the campground property with me at times and we talked.

On a warm, sunny afternoon, we sat around a picnic table and talked about God. I wanted God to give them an experience that would build their faith and trust in Him. The boy's attention was caught by a bird that was hopping around under a pine tree. It seemed to be wounded. His sister and I were alerted and we all made pursuit of the little creature.

As we neared the injured bird, it became startled and hopped into the brush out of our sight. After several minutes of searching, I wondered if we would ever see the bird again. As we continued the hunt, I began praying to God asking him to bring the bird to us if he wanted to use it to grow the children's faith. Taking a few more steps, I looked down at my feet to see the bird hopping toward my path. It was soon within reach. The boy knelt down and covered it with his hands and asked me to pick it up. I grabbed a hold of its feet and held the bird in my palm.

As I knelt beside the two young ones, I asked them if they wanted to pray and ask God to heal the bird so it could fly again. Both of them got excited and they offered up their childlike faith to God. I prayed with them and agreed with their prayers. Then I raised my arm opening my hand. We watched the bird fly away until it was out of sight.

I have no physical evidence, other than what I saw and experienced, whether that bird could or couldn't fly before the children and I picked it up and prayed for it. According to my sense of sight and touch in picking the bird up from the ground, it was not able to fly. But who am I? I am inclined to accept as fact that, *"...without faith it is impossible to please God, because anyone who comes to him must believe that he exists and that he rewards those who earnestly seek him." (Hebrews 11:6, NIV)*

Hope In The Lord

     Not long after staying at the dunes, I prayed and asked God to take me out of the country. I did not have a destination in mind, just a thought in my heart to go somewhere in search of the Lord and His purpose for my life. Two weeks later, a man from the local church asked my dad if I could travel to Costa Rica to stay with him and his family. He married a woman from that country and was moving there to work for the Lord. This man of God lent me some books about friendship with God which he had in his possession. His suggestion was to read and to study them as I prepared for this trip. My dad encouraged me to go.

     Through the process of learning about friendship with God, my interest grew in wanting to feel close to God. As far as I could remember, I had never felt close to anyone before. I put as much energy as I could into renewing my mind with the truths that were being revealed to me, hoping that I may somehow be transformed and learn to remain feeling close to the great and awesome God who had given me another chance.

     The feelings are still not always there. However, God continues to remind me that He is always with me, even when I do not feel Him close. Having the hope that I may someday be always able to feel His closeness gives me the desire to keep seeking Him. Persisting in my pursuit of friendship with God, I continue to renew my mind with His truths surrounding the fear of the Lord.

There must be hope in the fear of the Lord, if my heart is so inclined to seek after it. The NIV translation of the Bible records a truth which was revealed to me from the book of Proverbs. Chapter eight and verse thirteen declares: *"The fear of the Lord is to hate evil; I hate pride and arrogance, evil behavior and perverse speech."*

If I am going to live in the fear of the Lord, then I must set my mind to hate evil. I must purpose in my heart to not practice the things which sadden the heart of God. Where do I find hope to inspire me to have such an attitude?

The Bible is filled with promises which God has purposed in His heart to fulfill. He says He will fulfill them in the lives of men and women who choose the fear of the Lord, rather than lust and pride and all that is in this world. It is my prayer that God quickens His promises within the hearts and lives of all those who hunger for more than what this world has to offer.

Hope With Me, Pray With Me

These scriptures give me hope and have led me to these prayers. I pray as well that these scriptures would bring hope to you and inspire you to pray.

Moses said to the people, "Do not be afraid. God has come to test you, so that the fear of God will be with you to keep you from sinning." (Exodus 20:20, NIV)

O God, You have tested me again and again. Like a father who loves his child, You have disciplined me. You have never given up on me. May a spirit of the fear of the Lord be with me forever that, I may neither turn away from You nor break Your heart.

The midwives, however, feared God and did not do what the king of Egypt had told them to do; they let the boys live. And because the midwives feared God, he gave them families of their own. (Exodus 1:17, 21, NIV)

O God, I believe in Your faithfulness. Every soul is within Your reach. You have set me here for Your purpose.

Oh, that their hearts would be inclined to fear me and keep all my commands always, so that it might go well with them and their children forever! (Deuteronomy 5:29, NIV)

O God, You sent your one and only Son into this world to show me how to love, how to live. May Your Holy Spirit remind me of every word Jesus spoke; every act Jesus performed.

*The fear of the Lord is the beginning of wisdom, and
knowledge of the Holy One is understanding.
For through me your days will be many, and years
will be added to your life.
(Proverbs 9:10-11, NIV)*

O God, I have heard that wisdom comes from Your mouth. Speak to me Lord, speak to me. Give to me a discerning heart so I may hear.

*Although a wicked man commits a hundred crimes and still
lives a long time, I know that it will go better with God-
fearing men, who are reverent before God.
(Ecclesiastes 8:12, NIV)*

Have mercy on me, O God. I believe in You. Although I have not always acted like it, I do.

*So I continued, "What you are doing is not right. Shouldn't
you walk in the fear of our God to avoid the reproach
of our Gentile enemies?"
(Nehemiah 5:9, NIV)*

O God, nations have risen and nations have crumbled, but You remain unchanging. Do not let me waiver. Do not let me turn to the left or to the right.

Who, then, is the man that fears the Lord? He will instruct him in the way chosen for him. (Psalms 25:12, NIV)

O God, You have guided my steps since I was a child. Even when I have turned away from You in times past, You have not been far from me. You have shown me how to do what is right.

I put in charge of Jerusalem my brother Hanani, along with Hananiah the commander of the citadel, because he was a man of integrity and feared God more than most men do. (Nehemiah 7:2, NIV)

O God, all authority is Yours. You place men in authority for Your sovereign purpose. May the persons who You have put in order of authority over me be found with integrity and caring more about what You think than what they themselves or others around them think.

The Lord confides in those who fear him; he makes his covenant known to them. (Psalms 25:14, NIV)

O God, to hear Your voice is what I long for. You give me hope.

How great is your goodness, which you have stored up for those who fear you, which you bestow in the sight of men on those who take refuge in you. (Psalms 31:19, NIV)

All that I have is Yours, O God. I am waiting for You. Open up the floodgates of heaven and make believers out of all those who surround me.

*But the eyes of the Lord are on those who fear him, on those whose hope is in his unfailing love,
to deliver them from death and keep them alive in famine.
(Psalms 33:18-19, NIV)*

Where can I go, O God, that You do not see me? There is no place where I can go; there is no place that I can try to hide where Your Spirit does not see. Thank you for not giving up on me.

The angel of the Lord encamps around those who fear him, and he delivers them. (Psalms 34:7, NIV)

O God, may those who fear You in these last days be given the faith which Your servant, Elisha, moved in when he prayed for the eyes of men to be opened so they may see the angelic host You sent to help him.

Fear the Lord, you his saints, for those who fear him lack nothing. (Psalms 34:9, NIV)

Oh God, You are the great Jehovah. I learned a song down in Miami as I met with a church group whose families sprung from Haiti. I do not know who wrote the words to this song, but they are in my heart and I sing them to you now:

Jehovah Jireh, my provider... you are more than enough for me.
Jehovah Rapha, you're my healer... by your stripes I've been set free.
Jehovah Shammah, you are with me... to supply all I need.

You are more than enough... more than enough... you are more than enough for me.
Jehovah Rohi, you're my shepherd... leading me along the way.
Jehovah Tsidkenu, you're my righteousness... in all I do and say.
Jehovah Nissi, you're my banner... I have victory every day.
You are more than enough... more than enough... you are more than enough for me.
Jehovah Shalom, how I love you... God of peace is with me now.
Jehovah M'kaddesh, you're my cleaner... sanctifying, that is your vow.
Jehovah Shammah, you are with me... to supply all I need.
You are more than enough... more than enough... you are more than enough for me.

For as high as the heavens are above the earth, so great is his love for those who fear him;
(Psalms 103:11, NIV)

Sometimes, as right now in this very moment, O God, all that I know how to say is thank You.

As a father has compassion on his children, so the Lord has compassion on those who fear him;
(Psalms 103:13, NIV)

You are just, O God and You love justice; yet over sacrifice Your mercy triumphs.

Praise the Lord. Blessed is the man who fears the Lord, who finds great delight in his commands.
(Psalms 112:1, NIV)

In this moment, O God, how can I love You with all my heart, with all my soul, and with all my strength? Lead me in laying my 'self' down for others.

Blessed are those who fear the Lord, who walk in his ways. You will eat the fruit of your labor; blessings and prosperity will be yours. Your wife will be like a fruitful vine within your house; your sons will be like olive shoots around your table. Thus is the man blessed who fears the Lord. May the Lord bless you from Zion all the days of your life; may you see the prosperity of Jerusalem, and may you live to see your children's children. Peace be upon Israel.
(Psalms 128, NIV)

O God, You have searched me and You know me. You have heard my prayer and You know the poem in my heart which follows:

Will you walk with me and talk with me,
will you share with me your dreams;
Will you laugh with me and cry with me,
will you tell me how life seems?
Will you pray with me, night and day with me,
will you believe with me in God's Son;
Will you grow with me and show to me,
how I can be the one?
Will you share the sunlight with me, your whole night with me,
will you take from me your fill;

Will you be my best friend and be my lover,
will you say to me, "I will."?

Lead me in the fear of the Lord, O God, as I trust you to fulfill my dream.

He fulfills the desires of those who fear him; he hears their cry and saves them. (Psalms 145:19, NIV)

Teach me Your name, O God!

Do not be wise in your own eyes; fear the Lord and shun evil. This will bring health to your body and nourishment to your bones. (Proverbs 3:7-8, NIV)

Your way is right, O God! Shine Your light so that I may see how to live and move and have my being.

Through love and faithfulness sin is atoned for; through the fear of the Lord a man avoids evil. (Proverbs 16:6, NIV)

Neither have I been able to nor will I ever be able to make it on my own, O God. Pleading the blood of Jesus, I seek the empowering force of Your Spirit.

Humility and the fear of the Lord bring wealth and honor and life. (Proverbs 22:4, NIV)

Let me live, O God, to share what You have given me.

Charm is deceptive, and beauty is fleeting; but a woman who fears the Lord is to be praised. (Proverbs 31:30, NIV)

O God, may a spirit of the fear of the Lord be with the woman whom I will know as my wife one day. Clothe her with strength and dignity.

*The man who fears God will avoid all extremes.
(Ecclesiastes 7:18b, NIV)*

Grant to Your servant the gift of discernment, O God, that I may stay in balance and in step with Your Spirit.

*I will make an everlasting covenant with them: I will never stop doing good to them, and I will inspire them to fear me, so that they will never turn away from me.
(Jeremiah 32:40, NIV)*

Today in faith, I am holding You to Your word, O God. Inspire me Lord and in Your kindness be good to me. Share with me great and wonderful things which I have not yet known.

Then those who feared the Lord talked with each other, and the Lord listened and heard. A scroll of remembrance was written in his presence concerning those who feared the Lord and honored his name. "They will be mine," says the Lord Almighty, "in the day when I make up my treasured possession. I will spare them, just as in compassion a man spares his son who serves him." (Malachi 3:16-17, NIV)

O God, what can I do for you?

His mercy extends to those who fear him, from generation to generation. (Luke 1:50, NIV)

Thank you, O God, for extending Your mercy to my parents who raised me as best as they could to fear You. Continue to extend Your mercy to other family lines through my sharing of Your mercy in my life.

Then Peter began to speak: "I now realize how true it is that God does not show favoritism but accepts men from every nation who fear him and do what is right."
(Acts 10:34-35, NIV)

Thank you, O God, for all the people in my life.

What Is Better

From one man he made every nation of men, that they should inhabit the whole earth; and he determined the times set for them and the exact places where they should live. God did this so that men would seek him and perhaps reach out for him and find him, though he is not far from each one of us. (Acts 17:26-27, NIV)

To the living God, I pray: For those who are seeking the truth, O God, for those who are reaching out for You because You first reached out for them, make Yourself known to them in this very hour, in Your divine majesty, in Your great power.

As Jesus and his disciples were on their way, he came to a village where a woman named Martha opened her home to him. She had a sister called Mary, who sat at the Lord's feet listening to what he said. But Martha was distracted by all the preparations that had to be made. She came to him and asked, "Lord, don't you care that my sister has left me to do the work by myself? Tell her to help me!"
"Martha, Martha," the Lord answered, "you are worried and upset about many things, but only one thing is needed. Mary has chosen what is better, and it will not be taken away from her. (Luke 10:38-42, NIV)

In faith I have tried to sit at Jesus' feet. I've made many mistakes, but I keep finding myself being drawn to "what is better." One example of a time when I chose to not worry about a mistake that I had made and God worked it out is described below:

As the time for my high school graduation drew near, I began to be convinced in my heart that I needed to submit to some kind of authority in my life. At that time, I did not look to my parents for direction. I believed they were the foremost God-given authority figures which I had. But I did not talk to them. I looked to "Uncle Sam."

After enlisting into the Army and finishing all the initial training, I was given orders to be stationed in Germany. It was West Germany at that time. My buddy whom I had enlisted with on the "buddy system" traveled with me to the same country having like orders. We were given the understanding when we signed up that we would be stationed together. That did not happen.

Upon our arrival in the new country, we were both sent to different bases which were hours apart by train. I was less than happy, feeling betrayed by the authority on which I had depended. On the other side of the world from everything that I had grown up knowing and being wrongly separated, in my opinion, from my buddy, I had a big choice to make.

A phone call was made back to the recruiter who had enlisted us. The understanding I received was that because of the way things had come about with our orders, we could have chosen to return to the States and be done with our service. My buddy and I both decided to stay. Even though, I did not do so with my whole heart.

After the first three months at my first duty station, the First Sergeant was replaced by a man whom I had heard spent 18 years at the pentagon. Under his leadership my company seemed to me to start falling apart. That is how I felt which added to my uneasiness.

I gained rank and was given the opportunity to drive the Infantry Fighting Vehicle which I was assigned to. I did the best that I could to be all that I could be. I had not asked to be placed in the Mechanized Infantry. My desire had been to keep my boots on the ground. It is not recorded on my DD-214 discharge papers, but within the first year of service overseas, I was chosen as one of thirty men from my company to represent my battalion at a special training camp.

On the first morning of training, we broke up into squads and maneuvered through a twenty point obstacle course before running as fast as we could on a trek around the camp. I will never forget the fourth obstacle. It was two long logs like telephone poles lying parallel to each other. We had to run across them and jump off the end down into a pit. I led my squad through this one.

I safely made it to the far end and jumped down. When I landed, my knees did not bend. The nervous system signal from my foot, which had broken, to my brain must have been at least as fast as lightning, I imagine, because I immediately dropped to the ground. As I knelt in agony with my head down, I sensed a power source inside me that was not my own. Deep within my being an impression came to life in me, instructing me to stand up and help my squad so that no one else would break their foot when they jumped. I did so immediately and found the strength afterwards to continue through the rest of the course and finish the run around the camp with my squad.

When the race was done and my body came to a halt, I could no longer walk. Two men assisted me as I hopped on one leg back to the barracks. I was taken to the hospital to have a cast placed on my injured foot. At that time, a reflection within my soul reminded me of something that I was taught in my childhood. It was the words recorded in the Bible which Jesus spoke concerning the greatest love that there is. He said, "Greater love has no one than this, that he lay down his life for his friends" (John 15:13 NIV). I thought that is what I had done.

I became sad when I returned to the training camp as I listened to one of the Special Forces personnel talking with men from my company. What I thought I had heard him say is that he felt I was just crazy for doing what I did on the obstacle course. I may have been wrong but I felt as though I was being put down. I thought that giving up my self like I had done was what the Special Forces were all about; going above and beyond what is normal. I had always looked up to the Elite. Until that moment, I had always dreamed of being a soldier in the Special Forces. For a brief moment, I was able to live my dream.

In my heart, I attempted to hang on to thankfulness. I remembered back to the time when my graduation from Basic Training had drawn near and my platoon's Drill Sergeants called a company meeting to explain the "do's and don'ts" of our enlistment. One of my Drill Sergeants told my platoon to stay away from people like me who don't talk, don't show any emotion, and you just can't judge. I was thankful for the feeling that I had done something good by helping my squad which I imagined would have made my former Drill Sergeant proud. I felt as though I had proved that I was someone who could be trusted. But, I also felt as though it just did not matter to anyone else. After the special camp, I returned with my unit to the home base where I fell into a deep depression.

    I had enlisted into the Army to make changes in my life, to find a purpose to turn away from the drugs and alcohol that I had given myself to in my childhood. What I found was a greater freedom for my fleshly appetites to indulge themselves more readily. Upon enlistment, I had walked away in my heart from the authority which God had placed over me through my parents. Due to looking at my circumstances with the Army in a negative way, I walked away in my heart from that authority as well. The pipe and the bottle were what I had previously known and they welcomed me back. Depressed and angry, I accepted their invitation.

    I cannot rightly recall how many fifths of Tequila made their way through my system over the following months. What I do remember is awakening one night in my bunk, shaking in fear, waiting for the MPs to come and get me. In complete intoxication, I awoke that night from a dream though I believed that I had actually killed my First Sergeant.

That dream scared me to pieces. Deep down, I believed that I could kill. I was in a place where I was being trained to more effectively take another person's life. Through mind altering substances that I was indulging in, I was being deceived into thinking that I wanted to. Deep down, I knew that I did not want to wrongfully kill anyone. I began dwelling on how I might get away from the fears that were haunting me. Going AWOL was the one idea that came to me. That was the only one that I seriously considered. I waited until Christmas time and took a leave of absence to fly home for the holidays. I did not return to active duty.

It was less than one year later that I drove a car head-on into a semi. Even after all the miraculous events which followed that incident, I still allowed shame from my military past to weigh me down at times. I had turned myself in to the military after being absent-without-leave for thirty-one days and had been released, but I lacked hope. I did not understand how God could help me to see the mistake in a new light. Regardless, restoration began to take place in the summer of 1994.

I had been living for the summer in a pickup truck out in Lancaster county Pennsylvania. I did so as a type of mission trip to learn to identify with the homeless and to seek God's purpose for my life. While there, I was introduced to a group of young men in the church who were planning to take a trip to Mexico City to do some construction work on a church building for some friends of theirs. They decided to buy another ticket and take me with them.

After a successful trip, we flew back to the United States. Our return flight brought us back safely. It was at this airport that something even more amazing happened to me. While I was claiming my luggage, a man walked up to me. This man was a taxi driver who had been one of the men in my platoon over in Germany. He saw and recognized me and came up to talk with me.

I was told that after I had left Germany and had not returned, my company fell apart. He said that fifteen men from our company had gotten kicked out of the Army for different reasons. I am sure that to the majority that is not good news. But in a way, it brought healing to my heart to know that I was not the only one who was messed up.

Even though I had not handled my situation in the best way, I believe that God rescued me from something worse. Since then I have learned through the V.A. that I am still considered a veteran. I am not proud of the way I left the service, yet, the healing process has continued as God reveals to me over and over again that He is bigger than my past. I was given the opportunity to join the American Legion. I did so to show my support for American soldiers in the best way that I can at this present time.

There is no doubt in my mind that God certainly is much better. My heart continues to be convinced that God's purpose will prevail no matter where on this planet I might be. It is so much better to cooperate with God and join with Him in the work that He is already doing.

A Struggle For Power

In my youth, I looked at life as a game. In my eyes, at that point, it was a game that I did not have the power to win. At the age of fifteen, I wrote a poem for an assignment in my Creative Writing class. It was a cry in my heart that I hoped someone would hear. I received a D- for a grade and felt myself likewise as worthless. My heart cried out:

>Born innocent in the eyes of the blind;
>Unclean to the One who knows.
>Peaceful memories through the mirror of past;
>Soaking up the light.
>
>Corruption caused by fear;
>Shame by corruption.
>Night creeps up on the day;
>Yet never taking hold,
>For the sun must rise.
>
>Obeying the rules of the game being played;
>I felt adrift in the shallows of time.
>
>Just open your eyes!

When I wrote this poem as a teen, the pain in my heart was intense and I thought it just for me. Yet in this hour, a light shines through it to illumine a basic struggle which mankind has faced for thousands of years. It is a power struggle.

A while after the semi-accident, I worked in a trailer factory where an important episode of my life took place. God used an event during this work time to enlighten me about His basic principles of power. That God is all-powerful is the greatest of these.

I had heard stories of His power to deliver those He loved. They are recorded throughout the Bible. I had even experienced His divine power through His saving grace after the semi-accident. God's miraculous force was made evident in my life also when my head was crushed between the steel bumpers. But I was in need of experiencing His powerful message again in the present tense. The following example of God's work in my physical life reveals how the Lord brought spiritual deliverance deep within me.

I was bitterly angry one day. A scrap piece of metal had gotten tangled in my air hose. I bent down to retrieve the offending metal. I lost control. I angrily threw it through the air to get it out of my way. It flew through my right index finger and left a terrible gash on the palmer surface of the first knuckle. Rage consumed my soul as flashbacks of the real issues behind my anger passed through my mind. The bleeding was quickly controlled with bandages and I went back to work, but I held onto the grudge that had embittered me. I allowed the sun to go down on my anger. I allowed the devil a foothold in my life.

In your anger do not sin; (Psalms 4:4a NIV)

Do not let the sun go down while you are still angry, and do not give the devil a foothold. (Ephesians 4:26b-27 NIV)

The flesh wound quickly healed, but I could no longer flex my right index finger. The knuckle remained swollen for months and a great deal of pain reminded me daily of my anger. I sorely needed to examine my heart.

It was at this time in my life that I began to learn about certain powers that are in opposition to Christ. *"For our struggle is not against flesh and blood, but against the rulers, against the authorities, against the powers of this dark world and against the spiritual forces of evil in the heavenly realms." (Ephesians 6:12 NIV)* I studied the references in the Bible and found this partial list of unclean and evil spirits. The underlining is mine.

1) Bondage/Slavery-
For you did not receive <u>a spirit that makes you a slave again to fear</u>, but you received the Spirit of sonship. And by him we cry, "Abba, Father." (Romans 8:15, NIV)

2) Fear/Timidity-
*For God did not give us <u>a spirit of timidity</u>, but a spirit of power, of love and of self-discipline.
(II Timothy 1:7, NIV)*

3) Heaviness/Despair-
...and provide for those who grieve in Zion- to bestow on them a crown of beauty instead of ashes, the oil of gladness instead of mourning, and a garment of praise instead of a <u>spirit of despair</u>. They will be called oaks of

righteousness, a planting of the Lord for the display of his splendor. (Isaiah 61:3, NIV)

4) Infirmity-
…and a woman was there who had been crippled by <u>a spirit</u> for eighteen years. She was bent over and could not straighten up at all. When Jesus saw her, he called her forward and said to her, "Woman, you are set free from your <u>infirmity</u>." Then he put his hands on her, and immediately she straightened up and praised God. (Luke 13:11-13, NIV)

5) Jealousy-
…if <u>a spirit of jealousy</u> comes over him… (Numbers 5:14, NASB)

6) Haughtiness-
Pride goes before destruction, <u>a haughty spirit</u> before a fall. (Proverbs 16:18, NIV)

7) Divination-
Once when we were going to the place of prayer, we were met by a slave girl who had <u>a spirit by which she predicted the future</u>. She earned a great deal of money for her owners by fortunetelling. This girl followed Paul and the rest of us, shouting, "These men are servants of the Most High God, who are telling you the way to be saved." She kept this up for many days. Finally Paul became so troubled that he turned around and said to the spirit, "In the name of Jesus Christ I command you to come out of her!" At that moment the spirit left her. (Acts 16:16-18 NIV)

8) Familiar-
...Your voice shall also be like that of <u>a spirit from the ground</u>... (Isaiah 29:4, NASB)
And...
And when they say to you, "Consult the mediums and the spiritists who whisper and mutter," should not a people consult their God? Should they consult the dead on behalf of the living? (Isaiah 8:19, NASB)

9) Lying-
Finally, a spirit came forward, stood before the Lord and said, 'I will entice him.' 'By what means?' the Lord asked. 'I will go out and be <u>a lying spirit</u> in the mouths of all his prophets,' he said... (I Kings 22:21-22, NIV)

10) Whoredom/Prostitution-
"Their deeds do not permit them to return to their God. <u>A spirit of prostitution</u> is in their heart; they do not acknowledge the Lord... (Hosea 5:4, NIV)

11) Perverse/Distorted-
... <u>a spirit of distortion;</u> ...As a drunken man staggers in his vomit. (Isaiah 19:14, NASB)

12) Seducing/Deceiving-
The Spirit clearly says that in later times some will abandon the faith and follow <u>deceiving spirits</u> and things taught by demons. (I Timothy 4:1, NIV)

13) Antichrist-
This is how you can recognize the Spirit of God: Every spirit that acknowledges that Jesus Christ has come in the flesh is from God, but every spirit that does not

acknowledge Jesus is not from God. This is <u>the spirit of the antichrist</u>, which you have heard is coming and even now is already in the world. (I John 4:2-3, NIV)

I had read many of these verses before and had an abundance of intellectual assent to the facts. But I needed God to speak His word directly into my spirit. In humility of spirit, I had to seek Him continually until amazingly one day, He did.

On a night like any other night, I sought God in prayer. He turned my night into a night unlike any other. The truth that I needed was revealed to me through God's Word. I was convinced in my heart that when I had let the sun go down on my anger on that one night many months earlier, availability was given to evil spirits to work their destruction in my life.

It was not because I was angry. On a deeper level, though, I had held on to resentments and bitterness towards an individual person. By that one act in which I expressed my anger, a door was opened for an unclean spirit to gain access. I did not confess my bitterness to God, nor did I turn away from the bitterness in my heart. Thus I left the door open.

In God's plan, in His way, and in His timing, it was time to close that door. He showed me my weakness and then reminded me of Christ's blood. I then talked to Him about the wrong that I had done and asked Him to forgive me. I confessed my forgiveness of those who had hurt me. In my heart, I turned away from the hatred which had been settling deep within me. Looking down at my injured finger,

I spoke aloud the words which came alive in my spirit. God gave me the words to call the spirit of infirmity by name and command it to get off of me, in the name of Jesus. Immediately, I was able to fully flex my finger for the first time in months.

Though I could bend my finger again, the pain and swelling did not go away. Two weeks later, I was invited to go to a church meeting in a home. The man who had invited me to stay with him and his family in Costa Rica years earlier was back in the area. The meeting was in his parent's home and I was welcomed.

During this meeting, I shared the experience concerning my index finger. I asked the church there to pray for me as the knuckle remained swollen and painful. They did so and God had mercy. The next morning when I awoke, the swelling was gone and there was no pain. He delivered me as I sought Him. He healed me as I made myself vulnerable to share His good news and hold myself accountable.

Life is not a game any more. I am still powerless, though I do not have to attempt to win. Christ has already won. That is good news. For me to join in His victory, I simply need to humbly make myself available to Him in His plan, in His way, and in His timing.

The following list with Biblical references names a few spirits which work together with God for good. Again, the underlining is mine.

1) Wisdom-
*"You shall speak to all the skillful persons whom I have endowed with the <u>spirit of wisdom</u>....
(Exodus 28:3a, NASB)*

2) Humble-
*It is better to be <u>humble in spirit</u> with the lowly Than to divide the spoil with the proud.
(Proverbs 16:19, NASB)*

3) Humble/Contrite-
This is what the Lord says: "Heaven is my throne, and the earth is my footstool. Where is the house you will build for me? Where will my resting place be? Has not my hand made all these things, and so they came into being?" declares the Lord. "This is the one I esteem: he who is humble and <u>contrite in spirit</u>, and trembles at my word...." (Isaiah 66:1-2, NIV)

4) Meekness/Gentleness-
*What do you desire? Shall I come to you with a rod or with love and a <u>spirit of gentleness</u>?
(I Corinthians 4:21, NASB)*

5) Gentle/Quiet-
Instead, it should be that of your inner self, the unfading beauty of <u>a gentle and quiet spirit</u>, which is of great worth in God's sight. (I Peter 3:4, NIV)

6) Prophecy-
Then I fell at his feet to worship him. But he said to me, "Do not do that; I am a fellow servant of yours and your brethren who hold the testimony of Jesus; worship God.

For the testimony of Jesus is the <u>spirit of prophecy</u>." (Revelation 19:10, NASB)

The Apostle Paul's words of encouragement recorded in I Thessalonians 5:16-24 to the Thessalonian church in his day remain true for us today. *"Be joyful always; pray continually; give thanks in all circumstances, for this is God's will for you in Christ Jesus. Do not put out the Spirit's fire; do not treat prophecies with contempt. Test everything. Hold onto the good. Avoid every kind of evil. May God himself, the God of peace, sanctify you through and through. May your whole spirit, soul and body be kept blameless at the coming of our Lord Jesus Christ. The one who calls you is faithful and he will do it."*

In Search Of The Fear Of The Lord

I hope to always pray with the attitude of Proverbs 2:1-5 in my heart:

My Lord and my God, maker of heaven and earth, my Redeemer and friend, I have seen how desperately I need You; my need is to choose the fear of the Lord. I have lacked the fear of the Lord in many areas of my life. Have mercy on me and show me Your great compassion. I will seek You with my whole heart. As You lead me, I will follow. Teach me Your ways as I listen and observe. You have promised that if I accept Your words and store up Your commands within me, if I turn my ear to wisdom and apply my heart to understanding, if I call out for insight and cry out loud for understanding, if I look for it as for hidden treasure, then I will understand the fear of the Lord and find the knowledge of God. Bring Your Word to life in me, O God, so that I might live.

Here, I am with a teachable spirit, to learn from You. May Psalms 34 be a light to me in the days to come.

I will extol the Lord at all times; his praise will always be on my lips. My soul will boast in the Lord; let the afflicted hear and rejoice. Glorify the Lord with me; let us exalt his name together. I sought the Lord, and he answered me; he delivered me from all my fears. Those who look to him are radiant; their faces are never covered with shame. This poor man called, and the Lord heard him; he saved him out of all his troubles. The angel of the Lord encamps around those who fear him, and he delivers them. Taste and see that the Lord is good; blessed is the man who takes refuge in him. Fear the Lord, you his saints, for those who fear him lack nothing. The lions may grow weak and hungry, but those who seek the Lord lack no good thing. Come, my children, listen to me; I will teach you the fear of the Lord. Whoever of you loves life and desires to see many good days, keep your tongue from evil and your lips from speaking lies. Turn from evil and do good; seek peace and pursue it. The eyes of the Lord are on the righteous and his ears are attentive to their cry; the face of the Lord is against those who do evil, to cut off the memory of them from the earth. The righteous cry out, and the Lord hears them; he delivers them from all their troubles. The Lord is close to the broken hearted and saves those who are crushed in spirit. A righteous man may have many troubles, but the Lord delivers him from them all; he protects all his bones, not one of them will be broken. Evil will slay the wicked; the foes of the righteous will be condemned. The Lord redeems his servants; no one will be condemned who takes refuge in him. (Psalms 34, NIV)

Thank you, God, for hearing the song in my heart:

Here I am… looking back… over all that the Lord has done.
Here I am… remembering the days… when I used to say, "Lord have your way in me."
Here I am… once again… thanking you Lord for the work you have begun.
Here I am… now I am here… praising you Lord for the victory you have won.

> Here I am… gazing beyond… all my hurts and fears and hoping in a heavenly home.
> Here I am… to eat your word… forever to see the Lord Jesus on the throne.
> Let me hear the word of God once again…
> Let me hear your word alive in me…
> Let me hear you tell me who I am…
> Open up my eyes that I might see.

I have found nothing greater in this life than being in the center of God's will. There have been times, though, when acting by faith in the fear of the Lord has cost me many things. Like Joy Dawson reported in her book, "Intimate Friendship With God through understanding the fear of the Lord," I, too, have been misunderstood, experienced the loss of friendships, and suffered rejection of many kinds. But through every loss, the Spirit of God has remained true to help and to guide me. I have not always relied on this gift of God though I am convinced in my heart to seek Him more fervently today for His help and support.

There are different kinds of gifts, but the same Spirit. There are different kinds of service, but the same Lord. There are different kinds of working, but the same God works all of them in all men. Now to each one the manifestation of the Spirit is given for the common good.
(I Corinthians 12:4-7 NIV)

One of the gifts which the Spirit of God has presented to me is speaking in tongues.

He who speaks in a tongue edifies himself,
(I Corinthians 14:4a NIV)

I was once asked if I had ever received the baptism in the Holy Spirit after asking Jesus Christ to be the Lord of my life. At that time, I had not even heard of such a thing, let alone receive Him into my heart. I was asked if I would like to pray for this gift. I had recently awakened from the coma believing that God was real. I wanted all that I could get of Him. I quickly agreed.

The friend who had asked me, led me in a prayer of repentance and faith asking God to pour out His Spirit on me. He also asked that I might receive God's gift of speaking in tongues. I wanted it so badly, but all I could do is cry. He assured me that my tears were a sign that I had indeed received God's spiritual gift. He prayed that God would continue that work in me and help my confidence to grow so I could use it.

One week later, I started a class which I had enrolled in. During the beginning of the second week as I returned from school to the house where I stayed, I had a thought deep inside me to go out in the backyard and speak in tongues. For the previous couple weeks since my friend had prayed for me to receive the gift of God's Spirit, I had not thought about it. I was surprised when I felt directed from within to go out in the backyard. No one else was at the home with me, so I proceeded outside alone.

At first, I did not know what to do. I just started walking around the property. The sounds which my friend had made when he prayed for me weeks earlier came to my remembrance. They were nothing that my mind could understand. Thoughts of foolishness flooded my soul, but in faith, I opened my mouth and utterances began to flow from my lips which my mind could not comprehend.

For anyone who speaks in a tongue does not speak to men but to God. Indeed, no one understands him; he utters mysteries with his spirit.
(I Corinthians 14:2 NIV)

      Each day for ten days I went out in the backyard after my scheduled classes or events. Each of those days I spoke in what sounded to me as a different language. With each new experience of God's Spirit, my own spirit was encouraged and strengthened. May God help us all to be more spiritually minded?

Finding Direction

For the Lord gives wisdom, and from his mouth come knowledge and understanding.
(Proverbs 2:6 NIV)

If any of you lacks wisdom, he should ask God, who gives generously to all without finding fault, and it will be given to him.
(James 1:5, NIV)

More than twelve years after awakening from my coma, I worked for a building supply company. A part of the job entailed stocking houses and other types of commercial buildings with drywall. I had to carry a safe estimate of hundreds of drywall sheets each week for a number of years. The count for some weeks may have been in the thousands of sheets carried. Many of those sheets were carried up and down stairs. The bones in my arms began to ache. I believed that if I did not make a change in what I was doing that I might well need medical attention. This motivated me to learn how to give physical therapy before I needed it again. I had never imagined myself going to college. But this motivation was greater than my fear and I enrolled in my first college program.

After completing my schooling, I was given the opportunity to work as a Physical Therapist Assistant. I am now able to touch the lives of men, women and children who are in need, similarly, in some respects, to how I needed help years ago. Now, nearing two decades since the semi accident, the first hospital which I ended up at following the 'crash' has given me the opportunity to work as an associate to care for its patients. It is simply amazing to me that I am able to provide assistance to people in the same place where I once lay in a coma.

While attending my first college classes for Physical Therapist Assistant, nearly 20 years after graduating from high-school, I came across an interesting piece of material in the school bookstore. As I waited in line to purchase the supplies I needed for my classes, my gaze moved over the many copies of medical literature. My focus came to rest on a bar-chart, the only one of its kind in the entire school.

My eyes were fixed on this single 'helps' tool. It was so interesting to me. I began to imagine all the people I could help to find healing in their lives by practicing the principles outlined in the diagrams before me. My heart took a hold of the vision that I felt had been brought to my attention. Enthusiastically, I purchased the bar-chart. I hoped that God would help me develop the skills necessary to regularly practice this new gift called reflexology.

At another point in time, I asked my PTA program Director if she knew anything about the reflexology information which I had gotten at the school bookstore. She told me that the school does not offer any such classes and that she had no idea why that particular one was even there. My spirit was quickened and I trusted that it was there at just the right time for me.

With all the learning which was going on through my program studies, I did not put much time or energy into researching this new art. The term, reflexology, was new to my vocabulary. I just knew in my heart that I wanted to learn it so that I could help people.

Then, only a few weeks after I had made that incredible purchase, without my telling anyone about it or the excitement which I had for it, someone gave me a gift. It was an educational DVD on the topic of manipulating the reflexes in the feet. My excitement returned to me as I sensed fresh purpose.

At the next available chance, I drove to a clothing store and picked up a pair of socks that had individual toes sewn into them. I drew the diagrams for the reflexes in the feet on the socks with a permanent marker. I filled the socks with rice and then sewed them shut. I now had a pair of feet on which I could practice giving reflex therapy foot rubs. After finishing my school work each day, I practiced and practiced while watching and listening to the instructor on the video.

In a few days my confidence was growing as was a desire to try it out for real on a living, breathing human being. An idea came to me. I could begin by rubbing the feet of family and friends. I made mention of my intention to a few people in the church who I had been meeting with. An elder's wife agreed to be my first recipient. She had been having trouble with her breathing for years. Her doctor prescribed an inhaler to breathe-in a type of moisture so as to break up the congestion in her lungs. She used it every morning.

I was invited over for dinner. After eating together, we sat comfortably out in the living room and the baby powder container was opened. Since this was my first reflex therapy session, we played the instructional DVD. It detailed the position of reflexes in the feet in relation to the different parts of the body. I followed along, working with her feet. Nearly an hour went by. Then I heard a relaxed voice say, "I can breathe."

A short time later the elder's wife reported that the very next morning following the foot rub, she did not need to use her breathing treatment to be able to breathe that day. I was glad that her husband, as a leader in the church, sat with us and caught a glimpse of the technique on the video. I set out to teach all the church leaders and their wives how to better help each other through reflex therapy.

I decided to test my knowledge and skill with reflex therapy. I chose to give forty hours of service at no charge. If I saw beneficial results, I would consider the registration of my skills as a business. With the first forty sessions, forty hours of invaluable experience was gained. Many reports of improved health returned to me from family and friends who volunteered. It may have been my hands rubbing the feet, but God gets all the credit for the cleared sinuses, the broken fevers, the released head-aches, the regulated hormones and all the other wonderful results. It is truly a healthy touch.

It may just be a dream, but I hope to be able to someday have the financial stability to offer my reflex therapy service regularly to the public. Maybe someday my dream will come true. Whether my dream becomes a reality or not, my business will remain, "A Healthy Touch."

Thanks to those who perform the daily needs of building trailers, cutting glass and stocking houses with drywall, as I did for years. Thanks to all the people who have helped me along the way to get where I am today and to those who bear with me as I endeavor, to continue moving forward.

In his heart a man plans his course, but the Lord determines his steps. (Proverbs 16:9, NIV)

A Step In Obedience

When I first began working as a Physical Therapist Assistant in the town where I had grown up, my path crossed with a man who I remembered from my teenage years. I had no remembrance of ever talking to this particular person before. However, I started making a plan in my heart to do so.

At the first encounter with this gentleman, flashbacks of events from my childhood returned to me. I had wronged him all those years earlier and was being convinced in my heart that now would be a good time to make a confession.

When all the heavy memories returned to me concerning my past, I sought some counsel from a friend. This friend works as a detective for the sheriff department in the county where I reside. I figured he would know best how I should approach the confession which I believed in my heart needed to be made. I purposed in my heart to follow his good advice. Now, all I needed was for this one particular gentleman to cross my path again so I could do what needed to be done.

A few months passed by with no sign that I would ever be able to empty my heart of this burden. As I waited upon the Lord I was asked by the mother of a former therapy patient who I had worked with, if I would help her daughter as a personal trainer. I explained that I could not legally work with her daughter again as a PTA due to there being no script from a Physician. Nor had she been evaluated by a Physical Therapist. But I did offer my friendship to work with her daughter as a friend.

I secured a membership at a local health/training facility where the daughter had a family membership. We began working out at the facility together. One week after our initial training time started, I received a phone call from my new friend telling me that she would be unable to make our scheduled appointment that Monday. With understanding of the commitment she had made previously, I encouraged her to be free and take care of the business she needed to attend to. We planned to continue our workout plans on the next scheduled day. Even though I now had no reason in my own mind to go to the training facility that day, I still had a desire in my heart to drive there.

I did so without knowing what would take place when I got there. I began to warm up by walking on a treadmill. Moments later I recognized the man who I had all those childhood memories about months earlier. He entered the room and began using another warm-up machine. An impression came to life within me and I believed it was the Spirit of God telling me, "Here's your chance!"

I waited until the gentleman finished with the machine he was using and then I took a step of faith and approached him. I asked if I could talk with him. He recognized me and agreed. We walked out to a quieter place, away from the many others in the facility. I began by asking if he had owned a bait and tackle store across the street from the old Middle School years ago. I wanted to make sure that I was talking to the right person since it had been more than twenty-six years. He said that he was the owner of that store.

I then proceeded to tell him that one day when I was thirteen years old and, a student at the old Middle School, I had gone into the bait and tackle store. No one was in sight at the time and I noticed a handgun case was open. I reached over the top and through the back of the case to remove a .22 caliber semi-automatic handgun. I stuck it in my pocket and walked out of the store.

He did not respond immediately. I tried to explain that I was telling him these things so as to ask for his forgiveness and to offer remuneration for what I had stolen from him all those years ago. He mentioned that it was a big thing for me to come back after so long and tell him these things. He asked me, "Whatever happened to it?" He was speaking of the gun.

I explained that I had taken the weapon outside the city limits and had fired it on someone's property. After doing so I got scared and threw the gun in the trash. He expressed his hope that nothing bad ever happened with it. I offered a number of times to give him some kind of monetary reimbursement. Each offer was met with a silent decline.

Then he asked me a second question. "Did you learn anything from all this?" I was able to share with him that I was now able to confess wrong things I had done to people in the past. Without premeditation the words came to me that it was like a light turned on inside me; I found a measure of freedom through my confessions. He looked me in the eye and said, "Well, that's good enough for me," as he extended his arm to shake my hand.

      I believe God asked of me to confess to this man. My step in faith to be obedient to God showed me Christ's character in a more intimate way. It has brought a great freedom within me. It has enabled me to take another step closer into an intimate friendship with God. He showed me that I can trust Him.

      Several months earlier, I became licensed to legally carry a handgun. Though I had the state license and legal freedom to do so, I did not have peace within me to follow through with purchasing a handgun. In the fear of the Lord I followed God's directions as best as I knew how and was offered forgiveness by the man whom I had wronged. Having received forgiveness I now feel free to own and carry a gun. Acting in the fear of the Lord by being obedient to God's leading has brought a confidence in my friendship with God.

Deferred Hope

Ever since my third grade year, when I was selected to play the part of the prince who kisses the cheek of Sleeping Beauty in the class drama, I knew that I wanted to be close to a girl. Where was that one, special girl? During the summer after my accident with the semi, I cried out to God and asked him to cross my path with the one girl whom He desired for me to be with. In my own thinking, I could not make it on my own.

Not long after asking God to cross my path with the girl He desired for me to be with, I surrendered the outcome of that prayer to Him and went to a "Youth With A Mission" school. One of the students in my class was a beautiful, young girl from Pennsylvania. At one point during the schooling, she reported to me that she had a dream before leaving her home in Pennsylvania to get to the school. Before we had ever met or seen each other physically, she told me that in the dream she saw my face. When she first met me and recalled the dream, she was startled and amazed.

I tried hard to keep my mind focused on the things that I was learning about personal fellowship with God. After several months of feeling attracted to her, I finally tried to verbally express to her how I felt. She asked me to let her go, to just be free. I sensed that it wasn't the right time for a relationship.

In prayer, I asked God when the best time would be for us to get together. What I thought that I heard as God's answer was, "Six months, one year and two years after that." I went back home after the school. I purposed in my heart to wait for her.

We wrote a few letters back and forth. She continued to tell me to, "Just be free." I learned that six months after we returned to our homes from the school where we had met, she enrolled in another school. She mentioned that she planned to go there for one year. I waited in hope that what I thought I had heard from God was real. I only had to wait for two more years..., if I had heard correctly.

When she was done with her first year at the new college, she decided to return there for two more years. My hope grew as I waited. I tried as best as I could, while I waited and sought God's purpose for my life, to practice the things that I had learned about seeking God. Finally after the last two years were over, I spoke with the mother of the girl that I had been waiting for. I learned of the girl's marriage to another man. I finally had to let her go and try to be free.

For nearly the next decade, I looked for someone to be close to. Not one girl would even go out on a date with me. I had never been out on what I think of as an official date alone with a girl. Even to this day as I write this, I have not. When I was a freshman in high school, two senior cheerleaders asked me and the freshman quarterback to go to a school drama presentation together with them. That double date is the only date that I've had.

On my first and subsequent travels to different countries in Central America, I experienced the affection that the cultures there express to one another. I learned to kiss and be kissed on the cheek by girls and women in the church when meeting and parting company. I am thankful for those short times when I could experience affection and appreciation in that way.

When I was nearly twenty-eight years old, a girl agreed to go out to dinner with me. It was the first official planned one-on-one date of my life. She was quite a few years younger than me, but I was just looking for friendship. We set a time for one week, to go out to eat. When the time came, she was no where to be found.

The rejection I felt threw me back into my past. I went to a bar and drank so much Tequila that my body completely shut down. I ended up in a hospital emergency room. I was told that I had quit breathing. I awoke wondering why God keeps waking me up, but I kept trying to seek the Lord as best I could.

That same kind of episode happened again three years later due to rejection from a girl. I awoke this time, in a hospital emergency room again after my body systems shut down from drinking too much Tequila. I then purposed in my heart to quit looking for a girl to be close to. I keep waking up to find my heart being drawn to God. God has remained faithful, through all my trials and errors, to reveal His truth to me through His written Word. He remains faithful to show me that my ways are not His ways and helps me to return to His straight path.

When Jesus was here on the earth, there was a time when his followers asked him a question concerning marriage.

Jesus replied, "Not everyone can accept this word, but only those to whom it has been given. For some are eunuchs because they were born that way; others were made that way by men; and others have renounced marriage because of the kingdom of heaven. The one who can accept this should accept it." (Matthew 19: 11-12 NIV)

I have not yet been able to accept this word for myself. However, I am learning to accept that God's plans are greater than mine and His timing is better.

Precious

Have you ever done an internet search only to find hundreds of thousands of entries popped up in relation to the one thing you were trying to investigate? That very thing happened to me in the summer of 2004. I do not even remember the particular thing which I was looking for. However, I do recall feeling somewhat bored that day and I began browsing through the first few titles. One web page stood out to my soul. It had to do with pen-pals.

At an earlier age, I had been given numerous opportunities to write with several people in different places around the world. It had been years since I last heard from any of them as most of them had grown up, had gotten married, and had lost touch. I had a thought, with the entry of this sole web page, to look for an individual to converse with in pen once again.

A great many faces appeared on the screen before my eyes. But only one "about me" section found a place in my heart. With anticipation, I sent the required material to the couple who released to me the mailing address for this single woman behind bars. I wrote my first letter to her in faith. And in hope I waited for Amanda's words in return.

Nearly six weeks passed with no word. During this span of time, I was able to further examine my heart's motives and attitudes. Still single at age 34, I wondered if this was the girl in God's answer to my prayer. After thirty-four years of being alone, I figured I could wait a few more. It was simply amazing when Amanda's first letter did arrive.

Even from nearly eight hundred miles away, our hearts connected. Not long after we were indirectly introduced, I looked up the meaning of her name as a way to encourage her. A portion of the words describing what her name means became etched on my heart. "Precious gift" is a part of what I read. Now, to me she is "Precious."

When she was a twelve year old girl, her daddy dropped her off on a dirt road and told her to have a nice life. She never saw him again. During Amanda's childhood her mother was incarcerated. This landed her in foster care where she was raped by a foster parent. The governing authorities gave her an apartment of her own. It was during this period of time in her life, still a teenager that she was taken advantage of once again. But this time she ended up in a maximum security prison for something she did not even do. That is where we talked for the first time.

Our initial physical introduction was through a plate of glass with phones to speak through. I drove back to enjoy several contact visits with my new best friend. Her family also started getting more involved, taking time to visit her. Amanda started coming out of her shell. With encouragement, she enrolled in some college classes.

Several major occurrences followed in the year 2006. A big one was that she graduated from an optical lab. That made her so happy. She told me she felt as though that was the first accomplishment she had ever made. It was pure life to me, to be able to visit on her graduation weekend.

The biggest happening may have taken place later on towards the end of that year. During the previous year, we had been permitted to start talking on the phone. Near the end of 2006, she and I were speaking one night about her daddy. Our conversation focused on forgiveness. She stated that she had forgiven him, but that she never wanted to speak to him again. It was only one week later that Amanda called me. The first thing she said was, 'Guess who I talked to?' God brought incredible healing to her heart as she spoke with her dad for the first time in many years.

During her 2006 annual review in the maximum security facility, the leadership disclosed to Amanda that due to her conviction, she would never be able to leave the maximum security facility. When she relayed this message to me on the phone, I immediately thought about an elder's wife in our church. She had prayed for her brother who was in a federal penitentiary at one point in time. I had heard that God moved according to her faith and her brother's sentence was drastically reduced. This elder's wife asked me if I wanted to fast and pray with her for Amanda. We fasted and prayed for two weeks. One week later, I received a phone call and was told she had been given orders to be moved.

In the summer of 2007, I sent the following letter to the father of the boy who was killed in the incident which Amanda was convicted for. She had asked me to convey her broken heart to him.

Dear Mr. J.,

Amanda told me this past weekend, June 23, 2007, that you checked up on her at the FCCW a few years ago to let her know that you forgive her and to see that she was doing ok. She asked me to contact you. She wants you to know that she is sorry and her want for human words to describe the sorrow she feels for your loss has only been able to be met with tears as she longs to convey to you the depth of her grief. I too feel grief for your loss Mr. J….

After reading of your hopes and prayers for the females involved in the loss of your son's life, I was encouraged to move forward with my friend's request to get in touch with you and I had a sense to share some of my witness of Christ's work in her heart and life since I met her nearly three years ago.

When I met her, she told me she felt alone, not having any family contact in her life at that time. She relayed to me, like the newspaper clippings suggested, how her own father had left her and she had a state representative for a legal guardian. Since I have been close with her over the past few years, I have seen some wonderful changes. When I went to visit her at Christmas, 2006, I was able to meet her mother who visited with us at the same time. Her mother has become a solid strength for her over the past couple of years, as well as her older sister lending support….

It is evident that God is working in this young woman's life. In addition, upon my encouragement, we have begun to put a package of letters together to send to the Governor in hope that she will be shown mercy and granted an early release. Her mother has voiced a hope that possibly you would join their family, with others, in approaching the Governor to seek a pardon for her. I said that I would ask and I have felt encouraged to share with you some of what I am seeing in response to reading of your hopes and prayers for her. I ask with the mother of this young woman, will you join together with us in this fight?

Thank you for your time and heart to listen. Please inform me of any decision you make. You are much appreciated.

Sincerely,
DPG

    One month later, I received a special birthday present. On my birthday I received an email from the father I had written to. His words were extremely gracious and kind. He asked me to send a copy of his letter to my dear friend as well as to the other girl that was involved... and so I did. May God grant to them all the restorative justice of which he described.

Amanda my Precious

D

by David Paul Garty
2008

Amanda and I have shared a prayer together. We pray it often, if not every day. We pray not only for ourselves, but also for:
1) Our local, state and national authorities
2) Living Stones Christian Fellowship along with the church worldwide
3) VCCW and FCCW administration, officers and staff
4) The father of the boy who was killed, together with his family
5) Israel
6) Each one who will believe in Jesus one day
7) Our families and their families
8) Our friends and those who we may come into contact with

Our scripture inspired prayer follows in italics:

Great and awesome God, Father of the Lord Jesus Christ, our heavenly Father, pure and blameless is your name. Your character is set apart above all others. Your sovereign foundation of power come on earth as it is in heaven. Give us this day our daily bread. We need You, O God! Show us how and lead us in praying to You for the things we need, Jehovah Jireh, our Provider. In our silence, speak Your word, for man cannot live on bread alone, but on every word that comes from the mouth of God. Remember the blood of Jesus, O God, and lay aside our faults as we have forgiven those who have owed us or failed us in some way. And do not lead us into adversity, but rescue us from hurtful influences and all sorts of harm. Though, we thank you, Almighty God, for the trials of many kinds which do come our way because like You said years ago, the testing of our faith develops perseverance and when perseverance finishes its work, we will be mature and complete, not lacking anything. You are above all! All things are possible with You, O God! You are light and in You, there is no darkness at all! Thank You, God, for all of the people in our lives. Give us all the Spirit of wisdom and revelation so that we may know You better. Enlighten the eyes of our hearts to know the hope to which You have called us, Your riches and Your incomparably great power. Out of Your glorious riches, strengthen us with power through Your Spirit in our inner beings so that Christ may dwell in our hearts through faith. As we surrender to Your love, may we have power together with all those who believe in You, to grasp how wide and long and high and deep is the love of Christ. May we know this love that surpasses knowledge- that we may be filled to the measure of all the fullness of God.

Fill us, O God, with the knowledge of Your will through all spiritual wisdom and understanding. Open a door for us, O God, so that we may proclaim the mystery of Christ. Help us to proclaim it clearly and with great boldness. Your judgment is right, O God. By Your power, fulfill every good purpose of ours and every act prompted by our faith. May our love abound more and more in knowledge and depth of insight, so that we may be able to discern what is best and may be pure and blameless until the day of Christ, filled with the fruit of righteousness that comes through Jesus Christ- to the glory and praise of God. Be glorified, O God!

Near the end of the year 2008, I received a phone call from Amanda. I could sense the hurt in her voice. She described how her daddy had gone into an operating room for surgery and, during the procedure, lapsed into a coma. With love in her heart, she asked me to pray for the man who had left her on a dirt road when she was a child, the man she hadn't seen since.

Having the experience of being met by Christ in my own coma years earlier, I assured her that God was able to reach her dad. I also promised that I would pray in that way. The church prayer chain here joined me in that specific petition. Just a couple days later, Amanda called and told me what had happened.

The very next day after we had talked, she was given access to a cell phone to call her sister who was at her daddy's side in the hospital. She was able to tell him that she loved him. Her sister said it was like God was right there in the room from that point forward. Shortly after Amanda's words of love were spoken, her daddy was gone.

Two criminals hung on separate crosses on either side of Jesus when he was crucified. One hurled curses at the Christ. The other man expressed his belief in him. To the one who signified faith through his confession, Jesus told him, "...today you will be with me in paradise." (Luke 23:43, NIV). More than once it is recorded in the Bible that, with God, all things are possible. There is a strong possibility, in my sight, that Amanda will be able to see her daddy again, in heaven.

Near the end of the year 2009, Amanda and I started the process of putting a petition together for a Conditional Pardon for a reduced sentence since my first petition was denied a couple years ago. Amanda has worked hard to change her life and God has blessed her with many accomplishments.

We were told that Conditional Pardons are rarely granted, in fact less than 1% of them are granted in any year. Yet, we are encouraged. God has given us favor and help. The father of the boy who was killed in her case has agreed to write a letter with us recommending she be released early. The former Governor of Virginia and the Governor's personal contact from the Office of the Secretary of the Commonwealth have taken time to help us also.

It would be so awesome to be able to see God move the hearts of the governing authorities over Amanda that they would grant her an early freedom. It would be equally amazing if she and I could get together when she is released like we have talked about. Whatever happens, we will keep moving forward, we will continue to hold onto the truth.

The Lord reigns forever; he has established his throne for judgment. He will judge the world in righteousness; he will govern the peoples with justice. The Lord is a refuge for the oppressed, a stronghold in times of trouble. Those who know your name will trust in you, for you, Lord, have never forsaken those who seek you.
(Psalms 9:7-10 NIV)

A Moral Inventory

In his book, "Steps To Freedom In Christ," Neil T. Anderson has declared, "It is my deep conviction that the finished work of Jesus Christ and the presence of God in our lives are the only means by which we can resolve our personal and spiritual conflicts." I have come to this conclusion as well. Christ has met and continues to meet my deepest needs in this life. Actually feeling accepted, being identified in truth, having security and a measure of significance all have found their place in my heart through believing in God's Son.

It is not Anderson's steps that gave me new measures of freedom. But by confessing and turning away from any wrong actions, attitudes, words, and even thoughts that I may have been convinced of practicing as I meditated on the steps, Christ set me free. Together, the steps are an instrument by which I am enabled to submit myself more fully to God.

Submit yourselves, then, to God. Resist the devil, and he will flee from you. (James 4:7 NIV)

I understand that any freedom which I acquire must be maintained. Christ has won the victory. On the cross, He paid the price for sin and for death. When Jesus returned to the Father in heaven, God sent His Holy Spirit to lead us into all truth. By relying on the Spirit of God, I am making myself available for God to help me resolve my personal conflicts and those of a spiritual nature by renewing my mind with truth.

This moral inventory that I am engaged in has guided me to pray the words in my heart that follow.

Almighty God, thank You for being real with me and being with me throughout each day. Thank You for being here in this moment. You know everything there is to know. You have the power to make changes in any way You see fit. You are always present, O God. I am depending on You. I cannot do this on my own. I come before You now believing that Christ has all authority on earth and in heaven. Being in Christ by faith, I am purposing in my heart to share the good news of what Christ has done for me and to help others find the freedom Christ offers us all. I welcome Your Holy Spirit. Come and fill me up that I may walk always in truth. Protect me now as only You can and help me to prepare my mind as I record my family and personal history.

Father in heaven, make known to me the involvements which I have participated in with understanding or without knowing that have been cultic or with occult intent. Reveal to me the times I have been a part of false religions or under false teachers. In turning away from anything false, I will turn to You, O God.

Great and awesome God, I accept Your Word as truth. I am in need of Your revelations deep within my inmost being. I am seeking Your truth to set me free. I admit that I have been led astray at times. There have been many times when I have even deceived myself. Thanking You for the blood of Jesus and Your raising Him from the dead, I renounce my involvement with deceiving spirits and ask you to break any such bonds. In faith, I thank You Lord for being a part of my life. By faith, I now accept my position with Christ in heaven.

And God raised us up with Christ and seated us with him in the heavenly realms in Christ Jesus,
(Ephesians 2:6 NIV)

I understand that it is my responsibility to resist the devil. Thank You that in Christ by faith, I can do this. Holy Spirit, be my guide into the truth in all ways.

Search me, O God, and know my heart; test me and know my anxious thoughts. See if there is any offensive way in me, and lead me in the way everlasting.
(Psalms 139:23-24 NIV)

  Dear God, it is because of the abundance of Your patience and kindness that I am drawn to this change of mind leading me to alter the way I have previously thought, spoken, and acted. I have not always extended these same character traits to others when they have wronged me. There have been times when I have held on to resentment and bitterness. As I avail myself to Your scrutiny, dear God, please remind me of anyone whom I need to forgive. I will do so with Your help.

If you forgive anyone, I also forgive him. And what I have forgiven- if there was anything to forgive- I have forgiven in

the sight of Christ for your sake, in order that Satan might not outwit us. For we are not unaware of his schemes.
(II Corinthians 2:10-11 NIV)

Sovereign Lord, it is recorded that You said long ago that rebellion is as the sin of divination and insubordination is as iniquity and idolatry (I Samuel 15:23). There have been times that with my attitudes and actions I have wronged You with a rebellious heart. Have mercy on me, O God. In the name of Jesus I ask you to cancel all the ground that may have been gained by evil spirits when I acted in rebellion. Continue to enlighten my path that I may understand my rebellion fully. Lead me in turning away from this darkness. Help me to remain in the light of submission with the heart of a servant.

I call out to the living God. It is recorded in Romans 13:14 that You said long ago that we should put on the Lord Jesus Christ and make no provision for the flesh in regard to its lust. I must confess that I have given in to fleshly lusts. Thank You for your forgiveness. I receive Your forgiveness now and ask that You close any doorway which has been opened to the enemy to cause problems or disruptions in my physical body. I come to You seeking freedom from my bondage to the things of this world which I have participated in. Open my eyes to see how I have hurt You with these actions. I do not want to hurt You. I commit my body to You, O God.

Lord Jesus, I recognize that not all my ancestors were committed to You. Because godly principles such as those in Exodus 20:5-6 have been ordained in truth, it is possible that the sins of my forefathers were passed down to the third and to the fourth generations in my family line. With Your help in the name of Jesus, I renounce the sins of my ancestors. I renounce them and ask You to break any curses that have been placed on me due to their wrong-doing. I proclaim my new heritage in Christ. When Jesus hung on the tree, He became a curse for me. I plead the blood of Jesus and thank You God for drawing me close to You.

From Whence Didst Thou Come?

Therefore, if anyone is in Christ, he is a new creation; the old has gone, the new has come!
II Corinthians 5:17, NIV

    I remember seeing my dad's dad only four times in my life. The last occurrence, he was in his coffin. I do not recall ever talking to him, though there is a good possibility that I did. I was told that I stayed at his house for one week when I was a kid.

    It was made known to me at some time not long ago that my Grandpa was adopted when he was a small child. It was described to me that his biological father was from Scotland. I was told that my Great Grandpa, whoever he was, stayed for an undeclared amount of time in the United States of America while in the Scottish Navy. Apparently, he was ordered to go back overseas before he learned that his seed had impregnated my Great Grandma… whoever she was.

    A man with an Irish background adopted my Grandpa. This Irishman gave him his name. In faith, I am covered by the blood of Christ. Sharing in His name is what matters to me now. I lived more than thirty years before learning about my Grandpa. I am no different now than before I knew. I am still just a person in need of a Savior like everyone else. Thus ends my search for my family history.

My dad did not meet his biological mother until he had lived forty-one years. She is gone now. There is no personal recollection of her in my memory-bank. It was enough for me to know that my dad got to meet her before she passed on. My mother arrived on this earth an illegitimate child. Her mom was a sweet woman. It saddened my heart when she died. I was stationed overseas at the same time. Though I did not know her all that well, I did not get to kiss her cheek before she went.

My parents are enough history for me, as far as I am concerned. They met in Flint, Michigan where I was born. My parents raised me in the way that I should go. They taught me in the knowledge of the living God. I learned best from my parents when I watched them act unselfishly. While in humility, they considered those around them as having more importance than themselves. My brothers and I have parents who love Jesus.

My dad's story is greater than mine. When he was eight years old, he and one of his neighborhood friends rode around on his friend's bike to deliver newspapers. One morning, his friend asked my dad if he wanted to go to a church meeting with him and his family. My dad had never been to a church meeting before. After finishing the route, he went home to ask his dad and step-mom if he could go. They had been arguing. I understand that was normal. In the end, my dad's step-mom, the woman he raised me to love and call Grandma, beat his face.

He was in tears. He was not going to go to the church meeting, but his friend rode his bike over to pick him up. He decided to go with his friend. When they got there, the church people helped my dad clean his wounds and dry his eyes. Those caring individuals, who loved Christ, showed my dad something he had never known. For the first time, this street kid learned what it was to be loved. Everyday of his childhood, he lived with the experience or fear of abuse. However, God touched his heart through the church and he learned a better way.

Following active duty in the Marine Corp and eight years in a General Motors V8 engine plant, my dad was trained in pastoral disciplines. He devoted his life to serving God and helping people. To this day, he gives his time, his sweat, his blood, and his tears to share with others a better way. It has been a long process spanning many years for me, but I have learned from his example and have purposed in my heart to do the same.

On this journey through life, my own strength has not been enough. No matter how much or how hard I tried, I have not been successful in changing my own heart. Abandoning my 'self,' while walking through life's tests and trials is something I must do continuously each day while consciously committing all my life and will to Christ's care and control. With His help, I have been learning to choose a better way when the tests come. I can only thank God that there is no condemnation for those who are in Christ Jesus.

The empowering force which enables me to continue pushing forward comes as God's Spirit quickens His Word implanted in me. I have learned to renew my mind by searching through the Bible for the promises of God and personalizing them in my life. Availing the strength that I do have, I confess aloud and pray the scriptures in hope that the living God will bring them to life in my everyday experiences. I have grown to trust Him. He is faithful and He honors faith in His Word. From this have I come; to this I will go. May God bring His Word to life in you.

David Paul Garty (middle) with parents, Dave and Lin Garty.

References

1) Scofield, C. I., D.D., ed. <u>The New Scofield Study Bible</u>. New York: Oxford UP, 1984.
2) Zodhiates, Spiros, Th.D., ed. <u>Hebrew-Greek Key Word Study Bible</u>. Chattanooga, TN: AMG, 1990.
3) The Lockman Foundation. <u>New American Standard Bible</u>. Grand Rapids, Michigan: World, 1995.
4) BarCharts Inc. publisher. 2005 BarCharts Inc. 1105
5) <u>Reflexology Massage</u>. Goldhil Dvd. Naturaljourneys, Thousand Oaks, CA 2003 http://www.naturaljourneys.com
6) Anderson, Neil T. <u>Steps To Freedom In Christ</u>
7) Parkhurst Jr, Lewis Gifford. <u>The Believer's Secret Of Intercession</u>
8) Warren, Rick. <u>Celebrate Recovery</u>
9) Dawson, Joy. <u>Intimate Friendship With God through understanding the fear of the Lord</u>
10) Morehead, Philip D. <u>The New American Webster Handy College Dictionary Third Edition</u>. Eds. Morehead, Albert and Loy. New York: Signet, 1995.

Notes